Child Behaviour in the Early Years: Understanding Your Toddler

Karen Sullivan

For Cole, Luke, Joe and Ella and, of course, our resident toddler, Marcus

Teach Books Division, MA Education Ltd, St Jude's Church,
Dulwich Road, London SE24 0PB

British Library Cataloguing-in-Publication Data
A catalogue record is available for this book

Cover Illustration by Stephen Waterhouse

ISBN 978 1 85642 3458

Printed in the UK by CLE, St Ives, Huntingdon, Cambridgeshire

Contents

In this book the use of he, him or his is gender neutral and is intended to include both sexes.

Introduction

Raising and caring for young children must be one of the most difficult jobs in the world. Not only do children fail to arrive with an instruction manual, but they consistently challenge our expectations and experience with behaviour that can often seem completely inexplicable. Many of us become parents or carers with little practical understanding of the psychology of children; not surprisingly, perhaps, it is a subject that has perplexed and inspired researchers and scientists for decades.

Coming to it fresh, with an adult perspective and ideology, can make for tough times. Young children have their own way of seeing the world around them, and respond in ways that we, as adults, can barely begin to contemplate. Given the responsibilities we have to raise happy, healthy children – who will, one day, become adults, and key members of society – the pitfalls throughout the growing-up process can become worryingly important. If a child begins to lie or steal, will he become a criminal? If a child bites or swears, can we expect this behaviour to carry on into adulthood? What about children who won't eat and won't go to sleep, or refuse every effort we make to get them out of nappies? Is shyness a problem? Or will an inordinately cheeky child become a rude teenager? What is *normal*?

The first thing to remember is that every child is an individual and will come into this world with his own temperament and his own personality. Some traits are inherited, others are the product of his upbringing and other environmental factors. Parenting and childcare do play an important role in guiding a child through the early years and ensuring that a set of values and an understanding of appropriate behaviour are established; however, some children resist all attempts to encourage them to conform, and others are just, well, different. They take longer to understand and achieve things, or they whiz ahead so fast that the average parent's head is spinning. So, in essence, normal doesn't exist. There is no 'norm'.

That said, however, there are patterns of expected and acceptable behaviour, and there are boundaries within which this behaviour should be found. And, of course, letting things slip or ignoring problems as they arise can mean that actions just about acceptable in toddlerhood carry on into the older childhood years – when they are certainly not acceptable or within normal boundaries. And that is the trick to parenting a young child – working out where your child falls in terms of appropriate development and behaviour and then finding ways to adjust behaviours which could one day become troublesome. For example, biting is very normal in babies and toddlers at the young end of the spectrum, but becomes less acceptable as they head towards school age. I can categorically say that few teenagers and adults bite one another, so somewhere along the line the message that biting is wrong must get through. So while biting is within the norms of a young child's behaviour, it is still not acceptable, and it is our job as parents or carers to teach a child why – and to model and encourage alternative behaviour.

That's what this book is about. Based on years of child behaviour features I have written for Early Years Educator (EYE), it looks at the key problem behaviours in young children, assesses when, if and how they can be considered within normal boundaries, and what you can do to change the difficult behaviour before it becomes a problem. There are literally thousands of tips in this book, all of them tried, tested and based on the best and most current research. Your experience and your understanding of your child's individual characteristics will help you to make the best use of these tips. I'll also take a good look at discipline. Although young children may test the patience of the Pope, and spend most of their waking hours pushing boundaries, they do need discipline. Discipline not only makes children feel secure, but it also gives them guidelines for living which they will take with them throughout childhood, their teens and into adulthood. Getting the discipline policies right at home, and from a very early age, make the jobs of caring and parenting that much easier.

I have written about raising children for over 15 years, and most of my books have been published around the world, in many different languages. Studying developmental psychology also enriched my understanding of young children and the factors that make them tick. However, the single greatest contribution to my knowledge of young children has come from parenting three of my own (one of whom made a late arrival to coincide with the other two entering their teens), and caring for my partner's two children as well. Some things work according to the book; others simply do not. What you will find here is an amalgamation of theory and practice, which should make the job of parenting or caring for young children easier to understand and will lead to successful implementation.

Before embarking on the typical problems which feature in the lives of most toddlers and young children, it's worth taking a quick look at the normal developmental milestones. Understanding what your young child is experiencing and what he is capable of doing and achieving can help you to get to get the most from him – by setting realistic expectations, and encouraging behaviour that is appropriate for his age and stage of development. All children are different, and skills develop at different ages; unless your child is many months behind his peers, you have no need to worry.

Developmental milestones

At one year

- walks around the furniture competently.
- may walk around the floor on arms and feet.
- many can now walk alone (between nine and 18 months).
- drops from a walk to sit with a poorly controlled bump.
- picks up small items with a good pincer grip.
- gives and takes object from you.
- puts small blocks into a container.
- throws toys to gain attention.
- has a tuneful babble.
- usually says two meaningful words.
- turns when his name is called.

- starts to show an interest in things he wants.
- starts to show an interest in pictures.
- looks for a toy hidden under a cup and knows where to find it.
- holds out arms to help with dressing.

At 15 months

- usually walks alone with broad, high steps.
- can crawl upstairs.
- plays with wooden blocks and will post them into an open container.
- enjoys throwing toys.
- uses two to six words with meaning.
- babbles away to himself and to others.
- makes an attempt to feed himself.
- starts to climb.
- explores his environment with no sense of danger.
- is often frightened by loud noises.
- may be clingy and likes to be close to his immediate family.
- will eat a cut-up version of the family dinner.
- starts to show a dislike for wet or dirty nappies.

At 18 months

- walks well, with feet close together, and some flow of movement in his arms.
- runs.
- throws a ball without falling over.
- holds a crayon or a pencil and can scribble with it.
- uses between six and 20 words with meaning.
- understands more words than he can use.
- points to several parts of his body when asked.
- points to items in a book.
- starts to enjoy nursery rhymes.
- demands what he wants by pointing.
- is impatient and eager to do things for himself.
- likes putting things into containers and taking them out.
- pushes wheeled toys around.
- explores, climbs and gets into everything.
- likes to be close to his family and may be deeply suspicious of strangers.
- begins to imitate you – pretending to write, to wash the floor, to read, or to tell you off!

At two years

- holds on and can walk upstairs.
- comes down again on his bottom or his tummy.
- kicks a ball without falling over.

- turns the pages of a book.
- can do a simple puzzle.
- can build a tower of six or seven blocks.
- can copy a vertical line.
- talks incessantly.
- asks questions.
- calls himself by his name and gradually begins to use the words 'I' and 'me'.
- can put two or more words together in a basic sentence or command.
- plays beside but not with older children.
- Starts to pretend and to use his imagination.
- may begin potty-training.
- because of your child's growing desire to assert his independence, this stage is often called the 'terrible twos'.

At three years

- climbs well.
- turns the pages of a book one by one.
- is more independent and begins to focus more on adults and children outside the family.
- explores and asks about his surroundings.
- follows a two- or three-component command.
- recognises and identifies almost all common objects and pictures.
- understands most sentences.
- understands physical relationships ('on,' 'in,' 'under').
- uses four- and five-word sentences.
- can say name, age and sex.
- uses pronouns (I, you, me, we, they) and some plurals (cars, dogs, cats).
- makes mechanical toys work.
- plays make-believe with dolls, animals and people.
- sorts objects by shape and colour.
- completes puzzles with three or four pieces.
- understands concept of 'two'.
- imitates adults and playmates.
- spontaneously shows affection for familiar playmates.
- can take turns in games.
- understands concept of 'mine' and 'his' or 'hers'.
- expresses affection openly.
- expresses a wide range of emotions.
- separates easily from parents.
- objects to major changes in routine.

At four years

- hops and stands on one foot up to five seconds.
- goes upstairs and downstairs without support.

- kicks ball forward.
- throws ball overhand.
- moves forward and backward with agility.
- copies square shapes.
- draws a person with two to four body parts.
- uses scissors.
- understands the concepts of 'same' and 'different'.
- has mastered some basic rules of grammar.
- speaks in sentences of five to six words.
- tells stories.
- correctly names some colours.
- understands the concept of counting and may know a few numbers.
- approaches problems from a single point of view.
- begins to have a clearer sense of time.
- follows three-part commands.
- recalls parts of a story.
- understands the concept of same/different.
- engages in fantasy play.
- is interested in new experiences.
- cooperates with other children.
- plays 'mummy' and 'daddy'.
- is increasingly inventive in fantasy play.
- dresses and undresses.
- negotiates solutions to conflicts.
- is more independent.
- views self as a whole person involving body, mind and feelings.
- often cannot distinguish between fantasy and reality.
- goes up and down stairs without support.

At five years

- stands on one foot for 10 seconds or longer.
- hops, somersaults.
- swings, climbs.
- copies triangle and other geometric patterns.
- draws person with body.
- prints some letters.
- dresses and undresses without assistance.
- uses fork, spoon and (sometimes) a table knife.
- recalls part of a story.
- speaks sentences of more than five words.
- uses future tense.
- tells longer stories.
- says name and address.

- can count 10 or more objects.
- correctly names at least four colours.
- understands better the concept of time.
- knows about things used every day in the home (money, food, appliances).
- wants to please friends.
- wants to be like his friends.
- more likely to agree to rules.
- likes to sing, dance and act.
- shows more independence and may even visit a next-door neighbour by herself.
- aware of sexuality.
- able to distinguish fantasy from reality.
- sometimes demanding, sometimes eagerly co-operative.

Adapted from Caring for Your Baby and Young Child: Birth to Age 5, by The American Academy of Pediatrics, Bantam 1999.

Most importantly, however, try to maintain a sense of humour. Raising children can be tough and thankless on many occasions, and it will try your patience and test your resolve on even more. Keeping perspective, taking a step back when things become tricky, and seeing the funny side of the situation will always make a difference to how well you manage. And remember that the difficult times will always be balanced by moments of pure pleasure, an overwhelming sense of pride in your child, and, of course, a sense of achievement. Children love unconditionally, are enormously loyal, and instinctively want to please those closest to them. They learn through the examples we set, and if we are consistent and love equally unconditionally, they will eventually learn right from wrong, and understand the meaning of acceptable behaviour. They will always test those who are closest to them, because they feel safe in doing so – it is the primary caregivers who are most trusted, and therefore most often the recipients of trying behaviour. But look at it from the other perspective: the child you care for is experimenting, testing and pushing, learning about the world around him and what is expected of him, with the person he depends on most, and in whom he has the most faith. It's a responsibility, for sure, but perhaps, too, the greatest and most rewarding experience of all.

Chapter 1

The nuts and bolts of discipline

There is no doubt that today's children are more aggressive, disrespectful and violent than they were in years gone by. Teachers blame parents and parents blame the education system. Respect has become a rare commodity, and unruly children are the bane of many classrooms, households and neighbourhoods. Many experts and parents feel that a return to the Victorian age of corporal punishment would make the difference, and restore the balance of power. However, as history has shown over and over again, violence begets violence, and nothing positive can ever be learned in a climate of fear.

So what is the answer? A positive programme of discipline can make all the difference. Children who are consistently disciplined, actually *taught* the reasons for the importance of good behaviour, given an understanding of and respect for others and their needs and brought up with a sense of justice are much more likely to respond appropriately, and to become the type of citizens we all want to see. As such, they will have been treated fairly, governed with love and given guidance throughout their lives Not only does this programme begin from very early childhood, but it also begins at home.

Discipline begins in the home

I believe that discipline is firmly rooted in the home. Teachers and schools have a responsibility, too, but their role is more one of maintenance and reinforcement. The reason for this is that discipline is not about controlling children or laying down the law. It's about guiding children to adulthood, and investing them with respect for themselves and others. Indeed, giving our children self-respect is the linchpin to any healthy discipline policy and the key to empowering our children to make the right choices in life. One of the most important jobs a parent has is to teach life lessons to their child, and behaviour is part of that. For people to live together in harmony, there has to be a basic level of respect for others.

The role of teachers and carers

Many people whose job involves looking after other people's children find that they have what amounts to an almost impossible job. Some children are over-disciplined or harshly disciplined at home. In this situation, children often develop a need to exercise control away from their parents, and they become bullies, overly dominant, aggressive and resistant to anyone else trying to quash their spirit. Alternatively, they can develop a victim mentality, becoming attention-seeking, tearful, unable to make their own decisions and then heavily reliant on adults or other children. They may lack communication skills, and be unable to express emotions or needs confidently, largely because they have never been given a voice.

Other children are effectively left to their own devices, and have absolutely no understanding of the needs, rights, property and personal space of others. They may be out of control because they have never had the safety and security of regular and consistent boundaries. They may also be insecure for the same reasons. Under-disciplined children are as likely to become bullies as those who are harshly treated, because they feel neglected and have a need to show authority or importance in order to establish their self-identities.

So how do teachers and carers deal with the multitude of different children in their care? The most important thing is to set up a strong policy of discipline from the very beginning. Outline expectations, and *explain* why certain rules or codes of behaviour are in place. Rules are no good without explanations. No child has a divine understanding of the world around him, and every single little thing needs to be explained. For example, there is no point in shouting at a child for feeding his toast into the video machine. Why not? Seems like a good thing to do, and shows a little curiosity about the world around him. Has anyone ever told him *not* to do it, or why? The younger a child, the simpler the explanations need to be, but explanations there *must* be, or discipline will ultimately fail. Remember, discipline is not about power, it is about *guidance*. Teaching children how and why certain behaviours are acceptable, and others are not.

Even unruly children will respond to justice, and if your classroom or nursery becomes a place where they are treated fairly, where rules are well-established and clearly understood, they will become more confident and happier as a result.

As important as spelling out the rules is relaying the consequences of breaking them. Cause and effect is a hard lesson that even some adults find difficult to learn, but it's a key element of developing respect in our children. Pre-arranged penalties must be outlined as part of the discipline programme. Rather than being something negative, this programme actually gives children choices. They can choose to behave badly and have privileges revoked, or they can choose to behave according to the rules, and gain your respect, attention and approval. The vast majority of children seek approval from important adults in their lives, and most actually *want* to be the recipients of positive attention.

This is the concept of learned behaviour in action. Children who repeatedly gain approval, praise and the reward of time and attention when they behave well will continue that behaviour – particularly in the pre-school years. They may lash out and test their boundaries, but if those boundaries are firmly in place, they will eventually retreat to what they know makes them and their carer happy.

As long as your own discipline policies are in place, what goes on at home should not impact too heavily. Some children may be harder work, and resist your attempts at the outset, but in the safety of a peer group, and with the approval of a caring adult, good behaviour will result.

Chapter 1: The nuts and bolts of discipline

All children need discipline. It defines their world, and makes it a safe place to live in. They know their boundaries and they can express themselves and show some independence within them. Children without discipline are effectively thrust into the world without a guide, and they are forced to make decisions and choices that they are not equipped to make. There is a curious divide between the ways modern parents approach discipline. Many children are left to their own devices for long periods of time, and are expected to behave in an adult fashion, literally looking after themselves. Many of these children have far too much freedom without the guidance they need to use it healthily and successfully. On the other hand, however, some children are expected to behave beautifully at all times, and to achieve and succeed. With no personal freedom, these children are over-disciplined, with equally disastrous results.

Guidance

The best carers are those who allow their children some free rein, some scope to be children, freedom to be themselves, while still respecting the rights and needs of others. What children need is guidance, and an understanding of the world around them. This requires time and patience. Constant explanations are required to give children a realistic reason for why certain behaviours are unacceptable or disrespectful. They need to be taught the impact of the way they behave on other people. They learn to communicate, negotiate, compromise, make decisions, make choices, develop self-control, be themselves and take pride in who they are. They learn to live happily with other people when they are taught these lessons in the context of an unconditionally loving home.

Parents represent the first relationships our children have in their lives, and these relationships must be healthy and built on the sound principles of love, respect, care, nurturing, guidance, acceptance, understanding, communication, easy, shared expression, and, above all, security. Most of what our children do in their lives revolves around relationships and interactions – with friends, classmates, teachers, coaches, other family members, peers, babysitters, carers and even shopkeepers, authorities and virtually every other person with whom they come into contact. If they learn the lessons of healthy relationships and the ability to interact early on, they will be given the tools they need to find their place in the world.

All parents and carers need to provide their children with an understanding of how other people feel and think, and what will be expected of them in certain situations. No child knows instinctively how to behave, and, even with the best guidance, there will always be times when emotion overtakes logic, or exuberance overtakes wisdom, or temper overtakes self-control. And this is where patience comes in.

Today's hectic lifestyles are very much lacking in patience. Stress is a significant problem and impacts both on the time we have to spend with our children, and on the way we are able to interact with them. No one can exhibit patience when they feel exhausted, tired, fed up and powerless, and this has a dramatic effect on the way our children learn to see themselves. Our expectations tend to be high because we take our parenting responsibilities seriously, and often see any rebellion or bad behaviour as a reflection of poor parenting skills. We often lose a lot of the joy of parenting because we become overly caught up in the role of disciplinarian. And with that, we misplace our sense of humour, which is one of the best tools we have to negotiate the parenting minefield.

Control or teaching?

We do not allow our children to be children; we control rather than teach; we expect adult behaviour and decision-making in children who have little resources or understanding of what is acceptable or truly expected; we punish and penalise, rather than focussing on the very good things that are happening around us. The end result is that many children feel powerless, valueless, disrespected and unloved. They develop poor self-identities and never acquire the self-respect they require in order to be confident, conscious and caring members of society.

On the other hand, the emphasis on self-esteem in the past few years has caused parents to over-nurture, and to allow their children to get away with completely unacceptable behaviour in the belief that they have the right to express themselves and their unique characteristics. The result of this is, of course, that children become tyrants and they expect the world to defer to them. This is unhealthy for many reasons, but in terms of discipline, its impact is significant. Pampered children have no respect for anyone else and feel that they have an absolute right to have their needs met. Not only is this a dangerous viewpoint because children tend to believe that they are above or better than others and their accepted rules, but these children never actually develop self-respect. It's all too easy. Respect is earned. Once again, a child who is not invested with self-respect will never fully understand the concept of discipline and accepted codes of behaviour.

Parents' fault?

This isn't necessarily the fault of parents, who almost always have good intentions and the best interests of their children to heart. Some of the problem is societal, because mutual respect is underplayed in so many areas of life. Parents are also under huge pressures of time, and simply do not have the resources required to parent full-time. Extended families tend to be far removed, so the benefit of wisdom handed down across the generations is absent, and many parents have to rely on full-time carers to do their job for them. It's also difficult to be consistent when your resources are low and you need a little peace. Most importantly, children do not come with a guidebook, so many parents seek them out, and the amount of confusing information offered is often ambiguous. It's not surprising that many parents feel out of their depth and unsure of how to deal effectively with their children.

What tends to happen is a descent into what one Canadian doctor terms the 'talk, persuade, argue, yell, hit' syndrome, in which all attempts to negotiate behaviour end up with the same result – an almighty row and possibly violence born out of sheer frustration. No parent feels good interacting with children on this level. Children may be small and necessarily inferior on many levels, but this inferiority is something that rankles, and they want and demand a little power and respect. You think you are in control; they think they ought to be. The end result is locked horns, a power struggle and, ultimately, chaos. No one wins in these situations, and everyone goes away with bad feelings: guilt, frustration, anger, powerlessness and the lurking suspicions that they have no control over their lives.

We get the most from our children, and instil in them a sense of pride and self-respect, when we respect them and their efforts. Whether it's learned behaviour or behaving to attain the reward of attention and praise is irrelevant. The fact is that children learn to feel good about themselves, feel good about the way their behaviour is perceived and accepted, and thereby continue the behaviour.

A unique approach

There are many tried and tested techniques for disciplining positively and helping our children to adapt to their role in society. All children are different and require slightly altered approaches to daily discipline. However, the philosophy underpinning the techniques outlined in this book is suitable for all children, because these techniques celebrate uniqueness, they are built on love and understanding and they focus on the key element of discipline: respect.

The wealth of reality television programmes centred round parenting and dealing with unacceptable behaviour makes it clear that many parents and carers struggle to discipline effectively; they are often driven to distraction by unruly children who essentially rule the roost. There is one message that is abundantly clear from these programmes: for discipline to work, it has to be consistent and clearly defined. It must focus on mutual respect rather than control, and be based around the concept of guidance rather than punishment. Let's look at the nuts and bolts of a successful discipline policy, which can be applied to any child, of any age, in virtually any situation.

Avoid labels

Children who are labelled from a young age tend to conform to match their label. In other words, labels tend to become self-fulfilling prophecies. So if a child is constantly referred to as being 'fussy', 'difficult', 'naughty' or 'violent', chances are he'll live up to his label and continue the behaviour. The simple reason is that children believe adults implicitly and trust what they say. An important part of parenting involves encouraging children to like and accept themselves for who they are. In this way, they develop self-respect and respect for others. If they spend their childhoods living up to labels, they have learned nothing about themselves.

Active listening

Children understand quickly when they do not have their parents' full attention, hence the commonly heard cry: 'You aren't listening!' or 'I just told you that!'. And when they do not manage to get the attention they require through verbal communication, they will be determined to get it in other ways. A great deal of disruptive or naughty behaviour is undertaken simply to get some attention. If a child learns that being good and quiet gets them nowhere, you can bet they will raise a bit of a ruckus – largely because it always works. Even angry words and punishments are better than nothing. Active listening is an important tool for all parents and carers. It involves hearing what your child has to say, both in terms of the words he is using and the feelings between the words. It means asking questions, providing a real response to questions, offering words to help your child explain the way he is feeling, as well as a non-judgmental sounding board for thoughts, ideas and emotions. Children feel more secure when they can express themselves and know that what they are feeling is acceptable. They feel validated when they are given a respectful audience.

Apologies

Parents, like children, need to learn to apologise when they break rules and when they make mistakes. One of the problems facing society today is the fact that children tend to feel no sense of responsibility, and believe that rules or laws are not applicable to them. It's easy to see the root of this ideology, as they often grow up surrounded by a series of double standards, which is neither explained nor justified. When we apologise to our children, we admit that we have made a mistake, that we are human. Mistakes *are* human, and it is through these mistakes that we learn and grow. If we are unable to admit ours, our children will learn to hide theirs, which keeps them isolated and creates a fear of discovery. This not only undermines communication between parent and child (and all other authority figures), but prevents children from taking responsibility for their own actions, a fundamental component of respect and self-respect. Children also need to be encouraged to admit mistakes, to learn that people are often very forgiving when they attempt to make amends.

Choices

This is one of the key techniques for successful discipline, and prevents the horns-locked scenarios that regularly occur between adult and child. This technique involves offering choices, rather than giving instructions, laying down the law, or ruling by overly authoritarian means. It provides children with a sense of power, which is crucial to personal development. Life is about making choices – the right choices – and learning what happens when we choose the wrong direction. In a sense, this is the nutshell of discipline: teaching our children to choose appropriate behaviour and action. In order for children to learn the art of decision-making, they need to be given the opportunity to choose regularly.

Offering choices does not mean allowing rules to fly out of the window. Quite the opposite. It involves giving some scope for personal decisions within the structure of family or classroom rules and expectations. It gives the child some control over his environment and his own behaviour, and teaches him that there are consequences to his actions. For example, allow him to choose the way he behaves. In the middle of a temper tantrum, for example, offer a choice: 'You can stop shouting and screaming now, and I will be able to finish the shopping and we'll have time for a trip to the library. You can continue to shout and scream, I will be cross, and we will be too late to do anything other than go home. Which do you choose?' Give your child time to think, and then respond accordingly. Whatever you do, be consistent. If you say that you won't have time for the library, don't go. If you say that you will, you must make the trip.

Consistency

If there's one area where discipline goes wrong, it's here. Even with the best will in the world, adults become worn down by children – their negotiations, pleading, tantrums, tears and dogmatic approach to almost anything that arises. It's not surprising that we give in and allow the rules to slip, or a penalty to be relaxed, just to gain a little all-important peace. But one slip, and you've planted a seed in your child's mind: he gave in once, and he'll do it again. You can bet that the next tantrum or howl will be longer and more determined, because children know that they will, in the end, get their way. Moreover, where there is no consistency in discipline within a family or class scenario, children feel slightly out of sorts and less secure. Without the boundaries that rules and discipline create, they can experience moments of fear, and this is when they test and test those boundaries to make sure they are still there.

The bottom line is that consistency produces results. If children know where they stand, they are less likely to behave badly. If they know you mean business when you impose a penalty or make a decision, they will learn that the actions that led to this situation are probably unacceptable, and to be avoided in future. Consistency also involves imposing the same rules for *everyone*, and taking responsibility when any are broken. Make the rules, stick to them, and unless a well-reasoned argument proves them to be wrong, do not give in.

Creating an outlet

This technique may seem to be common-sense, but it is often overlooked. Our expectations are often simply too high, and all children need time and an outlet to be themselves, to explore their environment, to make decisions, to work through problems and, most importantly, to burn off a little energy and steam. Every child will have an ideal relaxing activity. Find out what your child needs to relax, and do your best to provide it. Sometimes all a child needs is some unscheduled time. Give it to him, and see what happens.

Decision-making

This technique follows on from the idea of offering choices. Ultimately, we all expect our children to learn to make the right decisions, but we do need to empower them and give them the space to practise. Sometimes they'll get it right, sometimes they'll get it wrong, but experimentation and learning from mistakes is part of developing as a human being. Too often discipline today involves setting down a series of rules and expecting them to be followed without a murmur. This is not only unrealistic, but it also teaches our children nothing. Childhood is a time of fun and experimentation, but it is also a training ground for adulthood. If children are never given any opportunity to make their own decisions, develop negotiating skills, plan their time and their activities, experience success and failure through experimentation and activities, and feel that they have some control over their environment, they will never have the skills necessary to deal with life.

How do you encourage decision-making? By offering some appropriate freedom. The point is to assess your child's individual capabilities, and to offer freedoms appropriate to them. It doesn't mean sending a child out unarmed into the wide world. It means providing, as your child grows, the tools for dealing with situations and experiences, and then giving him some space to experiment.

Emotional vocabulary

Children need to be taught to express themselves, and they need to learn the vocabulary to do so. Without emotional literacy, children are left to manage conflict, adversity and change in their lives with a limited emotional repertoire. They are, effectively, faced with inexplicable, confusing and even frightening situations and change that they do not have the tools to address or express. In terms of discipline, this can have serious implications. Children who are frustrated, frightened, under pressure and unable to express themselves, will undoubtedly need to find an outlet. This often manifests itself in the form of tantrums, anger, belligerence, tearfulness, whining and even rebellious behaviour. Regular communication is one of the keys to successful interaction and discipline, and it is something that children carry with them for the rest of their lives. If they are able to get their points across, verbalise how they are feeling and what they want or expect and make themselves understood, they have the tools they need to understand *themselves*. They also develop the capacity to understand the way others are feeling, which creates empathy for others, and, not surprisingly, respect. They also learn how to analyse why they are feeling the way they are, and often sort out their own behaviour long before you need to.

Expectations

Take a look at your expectations. If your child is frustrated, whiny, rebellious and even angry a lot of the time, look at what's expected of him. The chances are, he doesn't have enough time to call his own. Think too of what type of behaviour you do expect and work out if it is actually realistic. Remember that children go through a whole range of experiences on the path to adulthood. They are learning, in the process, to deal with emotions, understand their own feelings and those of others and to develop the art of self-control. Let them run off some steam from time to time. Let them show how they are feeling. If you expect too much from children, they will feel like failures because it will seem to them that it is never possible to win your approval.

The second element is to set your expectations, clearly and concisely. This can be done in the context of a meeting, where several people are involved, or on a one-to-one basis. It's a technique that works as beautifully in the classroom as it does at home, in the grocery store, or on the football pitch. At the outset of every day, term, week, match or whatever, make it clear to all involved what is expected. You cannot count on children to read your mind.

Explanations

Discipline is the art of teaching respect, and if you do not take on board the teaching element of the equation, you will never get across the reasons why certain behaviours are acceptable while others are not. Take the time to explain why you want things done a certain way, or why it is not a good idea to do things another way. At every opportunity, take time to explain what you expect, what others expect, and why. It's no good citing rules or saying 'it's the law' to children, because it doesn't give them any real insight into why a behaviour should not be repeated. You need to make it crystal clear. Stealing is wrong because it involves taking something that isn't yours, and it hurts the person who has been stolen from. Or running through the supermarket at top speed is annoying for other shoppers, because they don't have much time and they want to get through as quickly as possible, as we do, so that they can get on with the fun things in their lives. Some of the shoppers are older, and don't have patience for younger people. As boring or silly as it sounds, it does help to make clear why things should be done a certain way.

Family or classroom rules

Establishing expectations can have a dramatic effect on children's behaviour, and you will need to sit down to decide what is and is not appropriate. Focus on problem areas. For every rule, decide upon the behaviour you *would* like to see. For example, if you have trouble getting your toddler dressed in the morning, make it clear that the rule is no TV or breakfast until clothes and shoes are on. For every rule that is satisfactorily maintained, offer a reward. Obviously it would be impractical to give a treat for everything done properly, but there are many ways of rewarding children.

Remember that these rules will soon become a way of life, and you can drop them when children automatically comply with them. Rules will need to be updated constantly in order to be effective. There is no point in giving stars for getting dressed in the morning if your child has been doing it successfully, of his own volition, for a month. Change the rules, dropping and adding, as your child grows and develops.

For rules that are broken, a penalty will need to be determined. Encourage your child to choose his own penalty. You'll find that children are much harder on themselves than you will ever be.

Good behaviour focus

This may sound trite and even ridiculous as a disciplinary technique, but it works beyond all expectations. The problem is that most parents are so busy and tired that the only time a child's behaviour gets any real interest or attention is when it is unacceptable or disruptive. A child's mind soon equates attention with behaving badly. So why not change the focus. Instead of noticing everything that your child does outside the rule book, why not focus on what he does right.

Ignoring bad behaviour

This idea follows on from focusing on good behaviour, and is an important tool in dealing with children who continually seek attention or behave poorly. Ignoring bad behaviour doesn't mean allowing a child to get away with murder, it simply means turning a blind eye to antics designed to wind you up or make a statement. Allowing unacceptable behaviour to continue may appear to contradict sound disciplinary techniques. But most of the time children are attempting to get attention in the only way they know that will guarantee your response. By failing to rise to the bait, you are showing them that you will not tolerate their actions.

Major and minor: keeping perspective

One of the problems with today's disciplinary methods is that they tend to be heavy-handed. Punishments are meted out without regard for the severity of the crime and, not surprisingly, children feel a great sense of injustice. We've all heard the phrase 'Don't sweat the small stuff', and nowhere is this more applicable than in the case of raising children. If you nitpick, nag, cajole, pester and pick up on every little infraction, your child will soon lose interest and probably move onto bigger and bolder things. Little things simply do not need to matter. Minor infractions deserve a mention – but not even in every case. If you are hell-bent on picking up every single thing your child does wrong, you'll create a child who has no faith in himself, no self-respect or self-belief, and who feels downtrodden. If he can't ever please you, he'll give up trying. And that's a no-win situation for all involved.

Rewards

Rewards are effectively positive reinforcement. They give your child something to aim for, with the prospect of something good for himself at the end of the process. Rewards are not necessarily material goods or money; they can be stars which measure accomplishment, or extra responsibilities, freedom or treats. Stars or sticky dots of any nature may seem outdated, but for children they offer a very visual measure of their attainment, and they almost always work – in particular for short-term problems. Change the charts as soon as the new behaviour has become habit, or your child will soon become bored. If they lose interest, put them away for a while, and bring them out when the going gets tough. But don't under-estimate the power of rewards, even in the short-term.

Saying 'no'

Use 'no' only when you really mean it. And then do not alter your stance. Try to avoid constantly using the word 'no'. Try to avoid constant negative messages, such as 'Don't do that', or 'Stop!'. Children easily become bored by this litany, and soon begin to ignore it. And that's where the rot sets in. If your child learns early on, to ignore the word 'no', you'll have a much more difficult time re-establishing your authority later on. Save 'no' for the important issues, such as safety or extremely disruptive behaviour. The rest of the time, use diversionary tactics (changing the scene or focusing on another activity, for example) or a child-friendly explanation of why you do not consider what he is doing to be right.

Sense of humour

One of the things I find most frustrating about today's reality TV shows and parenting self-help books is that they consistently overlook the concept of humour. Parenting or caring for children is not just a hard slog. It can be fun, and very rewarding. It can also be very, very funny if you relax a little and see the humour in situations – for example, locking horns with a 2-year-old tantrummer.

No one can discipline successfully without a sense of humour, and using it is one of the greatest ways to diffuse a difficult situation. Much childish behaviour is, in fact, amusing. Rather than heading straight for the rule book and finding a punishment to fit the alleged crime, why not try taking a step back in order to see the humour in the situation. There is nothing wrong with laughing from time to time, and then pointing out gently that although it is funny, the behaviour should not be repeated because it is inappropriate. Then help the child to understand why.

Laughing and showing a sense of humour plays a number of key roles in parenting. First of all, it teaches children to laugh at themselves – to see that their behaviour is actually quite silly. Laughing at a child doesn't need to be cruel – and it is certainly inappropriate when your child is distressed or seeking attention – but it can introduce a playful element into your relationship, which helps to take the pressure away from a constant power struggle.

The power principle

This is a tricky element in all relationships. Every one of us needs power to some extent but it is something for which, if given a little, we can become overly hungry, and too much power can make monsters of the nicest people. Adults are in a position of authority, which gives them unquestionable power over their children. But it's extremely important not to abuse or misuse it.

Try not to be too controlling. Avoid power struggles, where both you and your children are hell-bent on winning. Because what is the reward? A little satisfaction? It's a short-lived commodity, and you'll be back at it again in possibly a few hours' time. This type of lifestyle is distressing and exhausting. Better to offer some choices, so that your child feels in control as well. Give a little power, so that your relationship reaches a more balanced and even footing. Only then can you communicate on level terms, negotiate, understand and respect. Over-control is disrespectful of your child, his views, his opinions and his way of doing things.

This does not mean relinquishing your role as mentor, teacher and carer. You will hold the reins for as long as your child needs you. But you will acquire his respect a great deal more quickly if you show that you consider him an equally important person. And when he feels in control, the lashing out, the revenge, the frustration and anger that drives so much of what we consider to be naughty behaviour, will be things of the past.

Time-outs

Time out is a commonly used punishment for a wide variety of offences, and there is no doubt that, for some children, it is an experience that breaks a cycle of frustration and fighting. But time-outs can also be a negative experience for many children. They are sent to their rooms, or to a 'naughty' chair or step, in an attempt to punish them. The idea is, I presume, that they will reflect upon their crimes and come back new and improved. The fact is that children don't normally work that way. Chances are they'll brood, plan a revenge attack, nurture bitter feelings, and feel a great sense of injustice. For young children, being sent away from the hubbub of the family or classroom can be soul-destroying, and they feel genuine anxiety that they are being left out or missing out on something important.

Time out can be a positive experience, if the goal is properly explained. If your child has completely lost it and cannot reason or see the reason behind a change of behaviour, it's a good idea to suggest a break. Not a punishment, but a chance to get away from it all. More of the 'why don't you go to your room, get out a book, listen to a story tape, play with your animals, listen to music, do some colouring?' variety, which offers an opportunity to calm down. 'When' – and this is important – 'you feel better and are ready to change your behaviour, you may come down'. Having a little fun time in his room does not mean that you are letting him get away with whatever crime he has committed. You are giving him the space to assess when he feels calm enough to *change his behaviour*.

There is no loss of face here, because he is in the driving seat. He chooses when he comes out, and he makes that choice when he is ready. Even adults need to learn when to call a halt to an unproductive encounter, such as an argument. And a little time alone serves that purpose beautifully. Your child will learn a life lesson through this type of technique. He will learn to monitor his own behaviour, and when things get past the point of no return, he'll learn that taking himself away for a little break will help to cool things down until he feels more able to cope. It's a lesson a lot of parents could do with.

Warnings and penalties

We briefly discussed penalties in the rewards section, and this is an important part of any discipline programme. Some people like to use counting: 'one' is the first warning, 'two' is the second, and 'three' means you're out. I prefer to use the footballing system of red and yellow cards. Yellow is a warning. Two yellow and you get a red. Red card means being sent off, or in this case, acquiring a pre-arranged penalty. This system works extremely well for children because it is so visual. Holding up a yellow card is a great way to stop an argument, a tantrum, a whining session or anything else that falls outside the rules. And it doesn't involve a whole lot of negotiation, emotion or useless words. They know what it means and they know what will come next if their behaviour continues. After a while, you may only need to call out 'yellow' or 'yellow card' for behaviour to shift. It's a little like programming your child.

How do penalties work? It's very simple. When you make your rules, set up some penalties which will be implemented when the rules are broken. Encourage your child to choose his own penalty. This system works for a number of reasons. Firstly because it gives children the choice. They are warned first, so they have the opportunity to change their behaviour. If they don't, they know what's coming, because it has been pre-decided. They cannot then claim that it's unfair, because they set it themselves. Secondly, because they have set it themselves, they will feel less of a sense of injustice (which tends to go with penalties or punishment of any nature). Finally, it teaches them behaviour modification. They have to learn – and fast – how to change their behaviour themselves if they want to avoid a penalty. This is a tool that will stand them in good stead for the rest of their lives.

If you are consistent, outline your expectations in advance, offer full explanations for these expectations, so that your child understands *why* certain behaviours are not acceptable, and your discipline policy will begin to take root. Praise the behaviour you want to see, and avoid offering attention for the naughty things. Offer rewards, freedom and choices to encourage a child to make decisions himself, and to develop respect for himself and others. Respect underpins all successful discipline, and if we can create respectful children, we have a genuine hope of stemming the tide of violence and unruliness that threaten our schools and society. What's more, your classroom or home will become a peaceful haven, a place of learning and development, rather than a battleground.

Key points

- Consistency is the most important element of all discipline.
- All children need to have expectations outlined, and reasons given for these expectations. Understanding the reasons why good behaviour is an important part of guiding a child to adulthood.
- Keep a sense of perspective and a sense of humour – don't sweat the small stuff.
- Offer praise and rewards for the behaviour you want to see, and use penalties sensibly. In this way, behaviour becomes learned and a part of everyday life.

Chapter 2

The Case against smacking

New laws on parents' rights to smack their children are currently being constructed, at the same time as 'reasonable force' is being allowed back into the classroom in order to control unruly students. It is becoming increasingly evident that many members of the public consider the return to corporal punishment in schools a necessity, in face of growing disruption; it's also clear that many parents defend their right to smack their children and believe that it is a justifiable and reasonable form of punishment. In fact, a recent television poll showed that 84% of parents were in favour of smacking. Let's look at the argument against smacking, and the very real ramifications it has on both children and society as a whole.

Against smacking

In 2002, I was the childcare expert on a BBC1 documentary entitled 'A Good Smack?'. I visited three families who regularly smacked their children and offered alternative disciplinary techniques. Two out of three families readily agreed to try my methods and not only did the smacking stop (permanently), but their children's behaviour and their relationship with their children improved dramatically. The other family made the decision to continue smacking as their 'final' resort punishment, and therefore saw no real change in behaviour. As a parent myself I am fully aware of the exhaustion, frustration and poor behaviour that can lead to smacking; however, I remain fully against this type of punishment for the many reasons below. Primarily, however, it is clear that a parent's job is to teach, not control, and while smacking might bring a quick resolution to bad behaviour, it teaches nothing at all. In my view, smacking equates to poor and lazy parenting, whatever its proponents say.

Defending smacking

I have been astonished to see a host of smacking parents defending their position in the media recently. Take one columnist in *The Daily Mail*, as a case in point. She writes 'It is an insult to the children who suffer real abuse not to make the distinction between reasonable discipline and wicked violence'. She believes that smacking is 'arguably a lot less damaging than the cold withdrawal of affection and approval which passes for discipline in many homes'. I'm not sure to which homes she is referring, but good discipline never involves the withdrawal of affection or attention.

On the same page as advertising *The Caring Parents Show*, Babyworld.co.uk features information on *How to Use Smacking Correctly*, quoting experts who claim that it can be used effectively in younger children to reassert authority, set limits, act as a deterrent to bad behaviour and danger and prevent trouble from escalating.

Parents themselves, on this website and others, claim that they are not proud of smacking (although, oddly, some parents use it as a premeditated form of punishment following a threat), and only succumb when they are tired or feeling out of control emotionally themselves. The defence seems to centre on the idea that because it does stop the unacceptable behaviour, it's a valid form of punishment.

One 'expert' claimed the other week that children never remember being hit, but can pinpoint harsh words instantly in their childhoods. Research shows otherwise. And ask an adult who has been hit as a child whether they can recall concrete or constructive lessons learned from the smacking. You'll usually find there are none – largely because they were too frightened to learn them.

Watch out, too, for the parents who claim that 'sparing the rod spoils the child', and use biblical ideology to defend their position. Huh?

What smacking really is

Many parents are outraged to have their gentle smacks or swipes labelled as abuse or violence. The euphemism 'smack' or 'spank' has somehow replaced the more emotive words 'beat', 'hit' or 'slap', and has, of course, diluted the impact of what is really happening. Make no mistake. When you hit another person, whether that person is a child or an adult, and even if your actions are premeditated or undertaken through exhaustion and loss of control, you are committing an act of violence. Try standing before a judge after lashing out at your neighbour or someone in the supermarket queue and explaining that you hit them because you were tired and they annoyed you – or try claiming that you had to do something to stop a situation from escalating. You'd get pretty short shrift.

The whole story

Consider this: the first relationship our children have is with their parents. If we hit the children, we are teaching them that violence is acceptable in a loving relationship. Children learn by example. If we smack them, we are teaching them exactly what we don't want to teach: violence, ignorance and hypocrisy. They learn quickly to do the same as we once did: first to submit to the more powerful person, to obey out of fear, and to hide the pain of being humiliated.

There is nothing positive about smacking. It is degrading, humiliating and often painful, and it creates negative emotions that form part of a child's emotional foundation. It's a faulty brick, if you like. Negative experiences and positive experiences make up a child's self-image. As parents we need to ensure that positive experiences are more plentiful, and that negative experiences become vehicles or opportunities for learning. Nothing positive is learned from being smacked (see below).

If you have ever been hit as an adult, you will remember feelings of rage, or perhaps anger, fright, distress or fear. You may harbour feelings of wanting revenge. Hitting is humiliating. It is an assault on our bodies, our integrity. How do you think hitting a child is any different, no matter what the circumstances? Can you remember being hit as a child? Can you think of anything positive about that experience? Parents are, perhaps, the only people in a child's life who love him unconditionally. What kind of love begets the emotions associated with violence?

Consider, too, the parents who claim they had to smack a child to teach him a lesson about safety – to stop him running into a road, for example. In fact, being smacked throws children into a state of powerful emotional confusion, making it difficult for them to learn the lessons adults claim they are trying to teach. Delivering a so-called 'good smack' may indeed serve an adult's need to relieve tension and anger, but at the expense of the child. While the adult's relief is temporary, the effect on the child is permanent. Smacking does not teach children that cars and trucks are dangerous. It teaches them that the grown-ups on whom they depend are dangerous.

The power of touch

The power of touch is well documented. For example, pre-term babies who are massaged thrive better than those who are not. Touch imbues a sense of self-worth. Touching someone is the ultimate expression of caring, affection and love. We know how good we feel when we are hugged, or stroked or patted. Children feel the very same way, and it gives them a much-needed security. When that touch is negative, done in anger, or to cause physical pain, it has extremely deep ramifications and it is a powerful way of saying that that child is something worth hitting, something unpleasant, and it imbues a deep sense of rejection and even self-loathing. No child can possibly believe he is worthy if his body is treated with deep disrespect.

This may sound over-dramatic and even emotional, but there can be no doubt that being hit is a negative experience. Research undertaken by Save the Children and the National Children's Bureau found that most children see smacking as any other kind of hitting and have negative feelings about their parents after being physically disciplined. Discussions with more than 70 children aged four to seven indicated that children felt smacking reinforced cycles of violent behaviour and did little to help build up a positive relationship between parent and child. One child said: 'You feel you don't like your parents any more' and another said: 'It makes you feel horrible inside'. The comments also showed that many children did not see much difference between parents smacking children and other forms of hitting. They compared smacking with being hit by bullies and realised they could not hit back when they were smacked because their parents could hit harder.

What children really think

The Save the Children and NCB survey drew startling conclusions from their discussions with children. Their consultation came up with nine major messages:

- Children defined smacking as hitting; most of them described a smack as a hard or very hard hit.
- Children said smacking hurts.
- The children we listened to said children were the main group who disliked smacking followed by parents, friends and grandparents; the vast majority of the children who took part thought smacking was wrong.

- The children said children respond negatively to being smacked, and adults regret smacking.
- The children said parents and other grown-ups are the people that mostly smack children.
- The children said they usually get smacked indoors and on the bottom, arm or head.
- The children said the main reasons children are smacked include: they have been violent themselves; they have been naughty or mischievous; they have broken or spoiled things; or because they have disobeyed or failed to listen to their parents.
- The children we listened to said children do not smack adults because they are scared they will be hit again; adults do not smack each other because they are big and know better and because they love and care about each other.
- Half the children involved in this consultation exercise said they will not smack children when they are adults; five year-olds most often said they will not smack children when they are big.

The effects of smacking

Studies show that many children who are smacked at home are more apt to be physically aggressive at school. They feel a greater need to gain power and therefore are more likely to be bullies, or use bullying tactics. But studies also show that some children do not necessarily turn that shame and anger into violence. They turn those feelings inward, and it makes them incapable of sustaining healthy, loving relationships.

Research has also consistently shown that severe or frequent parental use of physical punishment was associated with an increase in the child's aggression. Studies found that when physical aggression is studied directly (not, for example, via attitudes towards aggression) in older children, there is a positive association between use of severe physical punishment and aggression in the child. This suggests that severe physical punishment may contribute aetiologically towards the development of aggressive behaviour.

Psychologist Terry Luce is a professor at the University of Tulsa in the US, whose area of research is aggressive behaviour. Over several years of study he found that the more children are smacked, the more likely they are to be physically aggressive with siblings, in school and, as adults, with spouses and children. He says children as young as pre-school age will hit other children as a result of being smacked themselves. In teenage years, there is a high correlation between smacking and delinquency.

All smacking does is teach a child to 'Do what I tell you'. As a result, children learn how to avoid getting smacked, including lying and cheating, but not how to regulate their behaviour. They are less likely to internalise the difference between right and wrong or to develop a conscience. Longitudinal studies also show they are more likely to do poorly in school, and less likely to finish higher education.

What's particularly troublesome is that smacking is often done by otherwise loving parents. The message becomes, 'When you are angry with people you love, hitting is OK'. Therefore, when you smack you're modelling violence as an acceptable way to solve problems. This has an enormous impact on our society as a whole and may, in part, explain the huge problems we have with violence and lack of respect. Respect is, remember, a mutual commodity. If you are disrespectful of your child, you will never gain his respect. What's more, he is unlikely to respect authority figures in general.

Hitting children teaches them to become hitters themselves. Extensive research data are now available to support a direct correlation between corporal punishment in childhood and aggressive or violent behaviour in the teenage and adult years. Virtually all the most dangerous criminals were regularly threatened and punished in childhood. It is nature's plan that children learn attitudes and behaviours through observation and imitation of their parents' actions, for good or ill. Thus it is the responsibility of parents to set an example of empathy and wisdom.

In many cases of so-called 'bad behaviour', the child is simply responding in the only way he can, given his age and experience, to the neglect of basic needs. Among these needs are: proper sleep and nutrition, treatment of hidden allergy (many cases of behaviour problems are linked to allergies), and many children's overall health, development and wellbeing suffer from undiagnosed allergies, lack of fresh air, exercise, and sufficient freedom to explore the world around them. But their greatest needs are for their parents' undivided attention. In these busy times, few children receive sufficient time and attention from their parents, who are often too distracted by their own problems and worries to treat their children with patience and empathy. It is surely wrong and unfair to punish a child for responding in a natural way to having important needs neglected. For this reason, punishment is not only ineffective in the long run, it is also clearly unjust.

Punishment distracts the child from learning how to resolve conflict in an effective and humane way. As the educator John Holt wrote in *How Children Fail*, 'When we make a child afraid, we stop learning dead in its tracks.' A punished child becomes preoccupied with feelings of anger and fantasies of revenge, and is thus deprived of the opportunity to learn more effective methods of solving the problem at hand. Thus, a punished child learns little about how to handle or prevent similar situations in the future.

What does the Bible say?

'Spare the rod and spoil the child', though much quoted, is in fact a misinterpretation of biblical teaching. While the rod is mentioned many times in the Bible, it is only in the Book of Proverbs that this word is used in connection with parenting. In fact, King Solomon's harsh methods of discipline led his own son, Rehoboam, to become a tyrannical and oppressive dictator who only narrowly escaped being stoned to death for his cruelty. In the Bible there is no support for harsh discipline outside Solomon's Proverbs. Jesus saw children as being close to God and urged love, never punishment.

Physical punishment gives the dangerous and unfair message that 'might makes right', that it is permissible to hurt someone else, provided they are smaller and less powerful than you are. The child then concludes that it is permissible to mistreat younger or smaller children. When he becomes an adult, he can feel little compassion for those less fortunate than he is, and fears those who are more powerful. This will hinder the establishment of meaningful relationships so essential to an emotionally fulfilling life.

Discipline with love

Discipline is about teaching and guiding. It is about love and acceptance, not power or coercion. It is about providing children with the tools to make the right decisions in the right circumstances. It is essential, as it provides boundaries within which a child can be himself.

Physical punishment is about control and a need for compliance. These things have no place in a healthy relationship, either as or with children, or as adults. We need to teach our children to make choices about acceptable behaviour. We do not need to set out to control our children; indeed, no one has the right to control anyone. We need to teach by example, by showing and explaining, by reasoning and through love. When we smack our children, we change our relationship with them dramatically, and it becomes a power struggle.

The most effective form of discipline is through empowerment, rather than control – giving children an understanding of why discipline is in place, explaining expectations and making sure they are realistic, setting up rules for appropriate behaviour and giving plenty of praise for good behaviour. If a child learns that good behaviour is rewarded and that negative behaviour is met with pre-arranged penalties or punishments, he will make choices. That is, ultimately, what life is all about. Making the right choices.

The goal of discipline is to guide a child towards more responsible behaviour. Children need to use internal controls, through values, morals and decision-making. If we teach them that discipline comes from external sources, they learn nothing about themselves and about how they can control their own emotions and make responsible decisions. This may sound outlandish in the face of a four-year-old throwing his fifth tantrum of the day, or consistently repeating behaviour in spite of having been warned about it time and again. However, it's worth remembering that although a smack does get instant results, shocking a child into silence, tears or better behaviour, we have, as parents, missed a golden opportunity to teach a child something. What's more, the lesson they do learn will undoubtedly remain with them for a long time. Using smacking to discipline equates to disciplining through fear. We can see through history that most people do toe the line when they are afraid, but the negative feelings that are stimulated do not encourage happy, healthy citizens.

Discipline, like most aspects of parenting, involves work. It takes a lot more time and effort to spend an hour with a child explaining, reasoning, showing respect for feelings, explaining expectations and creating a moral framework for a child's life than it does to bring an instant resolution, albeit through violence. Studies show that most parents accept that discipline is necessary, but don't feel happy about doing it. Why then the contradiction?

In this book we'll look at how you can discipline effectively, and send smacking back to the dark ages where it belongs.

Chapter 3

Aggression

Bullying, rudeness and swearing have no place in the classroom, nursery or home. In spite of this carers, teachers and parents alike are finding that a lack of respect and verbal and physical aggression have become commonplace and almost accepted by parents and peers alike.

The plethora of violence in the media is undoubtedly to blame for the way many children behave, but when even two-year-olds have mastered obscenities that would make many of us blush, it is time to take action. While good discipline and teaching respect should be undertaken first and foremost at home, there are many things that teachers and carers can do to curb aggressive behaviour. Not all bullies are rude, and not all rude children are bullies. But the common denominator here is an aggression that must be addressed and re-channelled into activities that benefit a child, his peers, and the classroom or nursery dynamic as a whole.

The problem with bullies

Even very young children are capable of behaving like bullies, adopting threatening behaviour, using physical violence and verbal abuse to attain a position of power. Many of these children will go on to exhibit these behaviours throughout childhood and adolescence unless a concerted effort is made to ensure that the perpetrators understand that they are unacceptable.

Many children become bullies because they feel powerless. This gives them the authority they require to feel good about themselves and in control. Not surprisingly, many bullies are harshly victimised at home, or under-disciplined, or fearful because they suffer from low self-esteem. It is worth remembering that many bullies are, in fact, victims in other parts of their lives, and although they can be disruptive and irritating, they are worthy and deserving of care and compassion. To add to the confusion, recent studies have found that many other bullies have overly high self-esteem and that they are, in fact, the product of a generation of parenting that focuses on inflating self-esteem beyond realistic levels, and encouraging competition rather than compassion. So some of these bullies have an unrealistic view of themselves and believe that they are superior to others.

A 1978 study by Lowenstein found that teachers and carers tend to view bullies as hyperactive, of low IQ or underachieving. These types of labels do, of course, compound the problem of self-image and self-esteem in a bully.

What can you do?

First of all, it is important to teach bullies to empathise and to understand the impact of their behaviour. Many bullies have become hardened to abuse, having been victims themselves, and actually feel little or no remorse for their actions. This is largely because they have never been given an emotional vocabulary to express how they are feeling, and therefore use physical or verbal abuse to define themselves and their position in the classroom or nursery.

There are many excellent books for pre-schoolers, which focus on emotions. The 'Your Emotions' series, published by Wayland Hodder is a good start. *I Feel Frightened, I Feel Angry, I Feel Jealous and I Feel Sad*, all help young children to understand how they are feeling. Another series published by Wayland Hodder deals with values; for example, *Values: I Don't Care!: Learning About Respect.*

Make clear your expectations at the outset of every day, and ensure that all children understand that violence and bullying are unacceptable. Offer pre-arranged penalties for bullying, such as a short time-out (a minute for every year of a child's age is appropriate), or a few minutes away from a favoured activity. You should also encourage bullies to apologise to their victims. They will soon get the message. If you witness suspected bullying, immediately approach the child responsible, describe the negative behaviour that you witnessed, explain why that behaviour is a violation of expectations, and impose your penalty. Keep the conversation focused on facts of the bully's observed behaviour and do not let the bully pull the victim into the discussion.

Take time to explain why bullying is wrong. Sit the children in a circle and ask them how they would feel if someone kicked them, or shouted at them. Encourage them to respond honestly, and give them the words to do so – for example, did you feel angry? Hurt? Sad? Embarrassed? Ashamed? Little by little, bullies will see that their actions have repercussions that are not so nice, and they will also begin to identify their own feelings.

When you confront a child for bullying, do so in private whenever possible. A private discussion will remove the likelihood that the confronted child will play to the audience of classmates and become defiant or non-compliant. If you must address a child on his bullying behaviour in public, do so briefly and in a business-like manner. If you draw too much attention to the problem, the child will be getting attention and will continue the behaviour.

Give bullies power in a positive sense. Ask them to help you and praise them for positive interaction and help in the classroom or nursery. Give them regular responsibilities (feeding the fish, collecting the pencils, tidying the books), and reward their efforts (allowing them to choose the story, or be first in the queue at snack time). This helps them to see that good behaviour not only gets them attention, but makes them feel good about themselves. Encourage friendships between bullies and children who tend to be victimised, by making them partners for games, or asking them to work together on a project or a painting.

Rudeness and swearing

Once again, children who are rude often intend to gain attention, and to play to an audience. This behaviour is effectively a shock tactic, designed to attract an instant response from teachers or carers. And not surprisingly, as many 'naughty' children discover, it works. There are two elements here.

First of all, rudeness is effectively a learned behaviour. A bit like Pavlov's dogs, children learn that they get a certain response when they are rude, and will continue with this behaviour until they fail to get the desired response. Remember that all behaviours are learned, as children react to their environment and the people in it. As children interact with peers and adults, they learn ways of responding, reacting, and behaving in social situations. They also learn how others respond and react to their social behaviour. As a result, children adopt behaviours that appear to them to meet the expectations of others.

What children do is either reinforced or not reinforced by those around them. Acceptable behaviour continues if it is reinforced. Similarly, problem behaviour also continues if it is reinforced. Both kinds of behaviours can be extinguished if they are not reinforced. Many problem behaviours are continued because children are given attention when they behave badly. Many appropriate behaviours are discontinued because they are not reinforced. It's as simple as that.

It is also fairly obvious that being rude to carers or teachers is often considered to be breathtakingly brave and risky by peers, which feeds a child's sense of power, and gains him a circle of admirers. It is worth remembering, too, that many children are rude and aggressive as a result of watching violent media. In fact, a 2002 study showed that children who are exposed to violent media treat other children with rudeness and unkind behaviour.

The study confirms that violent media not only contribute to physical aggression, but break new ground in showing that the rude and crude behaviour in movies and on television is mirrored in the way children who are heavy viewers of violent media treat one another.

'This study asked teachers and students about how children in their class treated one another,' said study co-author David Walsh, PhD, the founder and president of the National Institute on Media and the Family. 'Those questioned had no idea how much violent media the other students were exposed to. What we found is that the children whom teachers and peers rated as the cruellest were the ones who watched the most violent media.

'The study also showed that as children grow older, the more violent media they are exposed to, the more they like it,' Walsh said. 'They become desensitised and watch more. Concerns about a growing culture of 'incivility' in society may be starting with our children.'

Swearing too, is a product of our society which appears to be lowering the threshold of what is acceptable. Even before the watershed hour on television, and certainly on cable channels, children are exposed to regular swearing. Older siblings, parents, sports stars and even children's sports coaches often swear regularly, so it is not surprising that children pick it up and pepper their own speech with expletives.

The worrying thing is, of course, that children really have no idea what they are saying, and how offensive it may be. And they soon learn that it gets a good, instant response from carers and teachers, so continue to swear.

What can you do?

- If you suspect that violent media is at the root of rudeness or swearing, talk to the child's parents and ensure that he is watching programmes that are appropriate for his age. Parents need to be much more diligent about monitoring children's viewing habits. Encourage parents (in a letter home, for example) to watch programmes with children, and explain why a television character's behaviour is rude and hurtful.
- Adopt a zero tolerance stance to swearing. Explain your expectations at the outset. Ask children to explain what the word they used means, and then encourage them to come up with four or five words that work equally well and do not cause offence. For example, if a child says that his 'bloody truck won't work', suggest that he use the word 'silly', 'broken' or 'useless' instead.
- If a child does swear, do not react with instant attention. Ignore the child (to avoid offering attention in response to poor behaviour), but focus on the activity. 'I heard an unacceptable word, and it offends me.' Explaining that swearing is offensive is the first step to eradicating it.
- Rude behaviour should be treated in a similar way. Do not over-react, simply explain why such behaviour is unacceptable in the nursery or classroom. If the behaviour is repeated, employ a pre-arranged penalty. Focus your attention on the positive behaviour you see, both in rude children and those who behave well.
- Make it clear that you do not have time for anyone who does not make an effort to meet expectations. After a time-out period, promptly go to the child and say: 'You may get up now.' Do not lecture. The child knows the reason for the isolation.
- To channel the child into constructive behaviour, you might suggest joining an ongoing activity. Praise the child as soon as possible for engaging in an appropriate activity. Channel extra energy into regular activities that will stimulate their curiosity and interest. Busy children are less likely to act up.
- Remember that children who are rude and attention-seeking may have learning or reading difficulties, or both. These make it difficult to understand and take part in activities. Not surprisingly, they become bored, feel stupid and misbehave. Hyperactivity is another potential problem, which causes difficulties with self-control, paying attention and following rules.
- If you have concerns that problem children may suffer from either of these conditions, draw it to the attention of their parents, and bring in any specialist teaching staff who might be available to diagnose and help.
- Inappropriate behaviours exhibited by young children stem either from patterns that have evolved in their past, or from a lack of understanding (caused by limited social experience) of what is expected of them. This is normal. With skill, adults can systematically change children's unacceptable behaviour to something more suitable.

Chapter 3: Aggression

The key to dealing with aggressive and rude children is to remember that they have learned this behaviour elsewhere, and received attention for employing it. By setting firm rules and expectations for your nursery or classroom, you can begin taking steps towards eradicating it. Give children an insight into emotions, so that they understand the implications of their behaviour. But also ensure that they develop self-esteem and realise that positive interaction with peers, teachers and carers will be rewarded – and, ultimately, rewarding. Bullies and disruptive children have often been the victims of harsh discipline or abuse elsewhere, and they require compassion and understanding rather than more of the same in your environment. Understanding motivation, and encouraging children to understand why they do things, will help immeasurably.

Key points

- Most childhood conduct disorders are learned elsewhere, and are not an indication that a child is fundamentally bad. The first step to eradicating unwanted behaviours is found in teaching children more appropriate conduct.
- Raising self-esteem and giving problem children regular responsibilities will help them to feel powerful in their own environment, and they will not have to resort to bullying or rudeness in order to get attention and gain control.
- A firm but consistent and compassionate approach will help children to see what is unacceptable.
- Encourage children to understand motivation and consequences, by providing them with an emotional vocabulary. There are a number of excellent books which focus on emotions and values, and they should be regularly used in the classroom. Try Hodder Wayland's 'Your Emotions' series – lots of different books, including *I Feel Angry, I Feel Frightened, I Feel Sad*, and much, much more. The same publisher produces the *'Your Feelings'* series, which includes many excellent books, such as *It's Not Fair, I'm Worried, I'm Shy* and *I Feel Bullied.*

Chapter 4

Anxiety

At various normal stages of development, most children experience anxiety and fearfulness which affects their ability to interact with others and to get on with the job in hand. Self-esteem is closely linked to feelings of anxiety, and there may be more at the root of a child's anxiety than you may think. Let us look at the various types of anxiety in children and examine the best ways to ease anxious and fearful children back into routine.

Children often display anxiety in the classroom or playground, or may worry excessively about activities that are occurring at school or in their childcare or nursery environment. About one in ten children have difficulties managing anxiety, but they can be difficult to identify as they are often very well-behaved and seemingly well-adjusted. Despite appearances, these children spend a significant amount of time worrying and avoiding situations of which they are afraid.

The consequences of anxiety can be sleeping difficulties, high levels of stress, physical symptoms such as stomach aches and headaches, and missing out on age-appropriate activities. Ultimately these children are at a higher risk of later developing problematic anxiety disorders and depression, and are less likely to live up to their natural potential.

What is normal?

Most of us have experienced anxiety or felt anxious at some stage of our lives and, in fact, through experience we discover that there is often no real threat and that we can learn to cope. A little anxiety also helps people to perform better, because it keeps them alert and focused on what they have to do. And some fears or anxieties can be positively helpful; take, for example, a child with a fear of fire. He is not likely to play with matches. Or a child who is anxious about swimming – chances are he will not be in danger of playing in the water alone.

The nature of anxieties and fears change as children grow and develop:

- Babies experience stranger anxiety, clinging to parents when confronted by people they do not recognise.
- Toddlers between the ages of about 10 to 18 months experience separation anxiety, and becoming emotionally distressed when one or both parents leave.
- Children aged two to six have anxiety about things that are not based in reality, such as fears of monsters and ghosts.
- Children between the ages of seven and twelve often have fears that reflect real circumstances that may happen to them, such as bodily injury and natural disaster.

Chapter 4: Anxiety

As children grow up their fears often disappear, or are replaced by others. Situations that once caused anxiety are replaced by other, newer challenges. So it is right to expect a child who is leaving a parent for the first time to be anxious; just as children starting school may feel frightened and unsure.

When is it a problem?

As normal as some anxiety may be, it can be considered a problem behaviour and be disruptive to a classroom or childcare situation. Instead of growing out of it, the opposite occurs, and the cause of the anxiety looms larger and becomes more prevalent. The anxiety becomes a phobia, or a fear that is extreme, severe and persistent.

When focusing on a child's anxieties, ask yourself whether the fear and the behaviour a child is exhibiting is typical for his age. If it is, it is a good bet that his fears will resolve before they become serious cause for concern. This is not to say that the anxiety should be discounted or ignored; rather, it should be considered as a factor in the child's normal development.

When anxiety is long-standing, it is worth considering issues of self-esteem, or looking at ways to address the cause of the anxiety. In either case, it is necessary to involve parents in the overall picture, and develop a strategy to work together.

Symptoms of anxiety

Anxiety can manifest itself in many ways, including a child who:

- is exceptionally well behaved: never in trouble, always follows instructions, may appear bossy when it comes to getting peers to stick to rules and routines.
- asks many unnecessary questions or never asks questions.
- becomes upset when a mistake is made or if there is a change of routine (such as a sports class, a lunch break or a substitute teacher).
- does not, or is slow to, complete work because he gets stuck trying to get the right answer or a perfectly presented page or piece of artwork.
- is a loner or restricted to a small group of safe people (younger or older).
- becomes ill when performances are necessary (may be absent).
- may blush, shake or mumble when answering questions or giving presentations.
- becomes distressed if a particular friend is not at school or at an activity.
- has difficulty separating from parents at the beginning of the day or is clingy when a parent is at school.
- worries towards the end of the day about parents being there to collect him.
- has difficulty settling at the beginning of each term or perhaps each Monday (parents may be the only witnesses of this).
- avoids eye contact with teachers or peers.
- appears unhappy, always finding a potential danger in a situation.

So what is the answer?

The first and most important thing that all teachers and carers can do is to establish regular communication with parents, to ascertain whether there is anything particular in your environment that is causing anxiety, or whether there is a problem at home that might be exacerbating the issue.

Practical tips for teachers

- Provide support and encouragement, but without too much fuss. In other words, acknowledge the problem ('I can see you are frightened'), but also show some acceptance and belief that they can get through it ('Try the best you can'; 'It's always hard the first time'). Do not focus overly on the issues. Just make it clear that you understand the problem and you are confident of the child's ability to master it.
- Reward non-anxious behaviour and ignore anxious behaviours – reward a child who answers a question voluntarily for the first time but overlook a child who begins to get weepy when they have to change classrooms or activities.
- Encourage risk-taking in small steps by establishing a set of challenges to help children overcome a particular fear – such as coming into a classroom alone (a little further each day), or answering a question in front of more and more people, rewarding each attempt.
- Provide opportunities for developing independence – ask anxious children to run messages or distribute art supplies.
- Ask them an occasional 'easy' question but do not push them if they do not answer.
- Allow them to experience the natural consequences of their fears.
- Do not treat anxious behaviour as naughtiness – they are not being deliberately difficult.
- Discuss your perceptions with parents. Is this child also worrying at home? If so, seek help from your local authority, or encourage parents to talk to their GP.
- Plan for a shortened day during the first few days of school or nursery. This allows children to gradually adjust to being away from their parents and gives them time to learn classroom routines.
- Set guidelines with parents regarding separation. For example, some parents may try to quietly leave the room while their child is occupied. While this may make it easier for the parent to get away, it may increase anxiety for the child whose parent has suddenly disappeared.
- Display duplicates of popular items. This encourages parallel play as pre-school children become acquainted with one another and reduces competition for particular materials.
- Expect some tears. Reassure parents that this is typical. By staying calm and conveying a matter-of-fact, upbeat manner, early childhood teachers convey to both children and parents that it is okay to cry, but everything will be fine.
- Establish a routine. Pre-school and reception-aged children feel much more secure when they can anticipate what is coming next in their day. Children quickly remember the schedule and handle transitions more easily.
- Plan for smooth transitions. Transitions between activities are the hardest part of the day for both children and teachers. By moving pre-school children in small groups, perhaps by singing a familiar song with each child's name in it, teachers can avoid the stress of trying to move an entire class of young children.

Practical tips for carers

- Recognise that the fear is real. As trivial as it may seem, it feels real to the child and it is causing him to feel anxious. Words often take some of the power out of emotion; if you can give the fear a name it becomes more manageable. The more you talk about a negative feeling the less powerful it becomes.
- Never belittle the fear as a way of forcing the child to overcome it. Telling a child, 'Don't be ridiculous! There are no monsters in your cupboard!' will not make the fear go away.
- However, do not cater to fears. If your child does not like dogs, do not cross the street to avoid one, which reinforces the notion that dogs should be feared.
- Teach coping strategies. For instance, using you as home base, the child can venture out toward the feared object and then return to you for safety before venturing out again. The child can also learn some positive self-statements, such as 'I can do this' and 'I will be okay'.
- Stick to routines, which will help an anxious child feel more secure.
- Listen to a child's concerns, and let him see that you are taking steps to address his expressed needs in your planning and expectations. During your conversations about his concerns, you can give him practical information to counteract irrational fears and worries.
- Realise that children's anxiety may be expressed through behaviours such as aggression, tantrums, defiance or avoiding school. Always consider anxiety as a cause when a child exhibits negative behaviour.

The link with self-esteem

Healthy self-esteem is a child's armour against the challenges of the world. Children who feel good about themselves seem to have an easier time handling conflicts and resisting negative pressures. They tend to smile more readily and enjoy life. They are also realistic and generally optimistic.

In contrast, for children who have low self-esteem, challenges can become sources of major anxiety and frustration. Children who think poorly of themselves have a hard time finding solutions to problems. If they are plagued by self-critical thoughts, such as 'I'm no good' or 'I can't do anything right', they may become passive, withdrawn or depressed. Faced with a new challenge, their immediate response is 'I can't'.

Creating healthy self-esteem

- Watch what you say. Children are very sensitive to what adults say to them. Remember to praise effort as well as achievement, but be truthful, or the praise will become meaningless.
- Discipline is important. An undisciplined child will inevitably grow up with poor self-esteem. He will encounter rules and regulations and will find it very difficult to conform if his parents have not regulated his behaviour. An undisciplined child will probably have no respect either for his parents, or for those in positions of authority. As a result he will often find himself in trouble and the resulting chastisement will lower his self-esteem further. Remember that poor self-esteem is not a child's fault. If you stick to a

firm routine and outline your expectations in advance, even the most unruly child will learn to feel more secure in the context of a disciplined environment.
- Encourage children to become involved in constructive experiences. Activities which encourage co-operation, rather than competition, are especially helpful in fostering self-esteem. For example, mentoring programmes in which an older child helps a younger one learn to read can do wonders for both children.
- Build on a child's positive aspects and talents, rather than focusing on what they cannot do. Constant criticism destroys self-esteem.
- Listen to the child. If a child is ignored, he may act badly to attract attention to himself, or else may become withdrawn, believing that he is not important enough for anyone to take notice of him.
- Asking for a child's opinion on an issue makes him feel valued and important.
- Teach children to respect others' differences and weaknesses and not to make harsh judgements.
- Help children to plan and set goals, however small. Achieving a goal is a positive event, which helps to build self-esteem and also shows a child that he has some sort of control in his life.

For the majority of children, anxiety and fear are normal parts of development. With a little imagination, patience and acceptance, these anxieties can be gently overcome. What is important, however, is for carers and teachers to recognise when anxiety is at the root of problem behaviour. Encouraging children to express themselves verbally and teaching them that fears are normal, while taking steps to build their self-esteem, will make most anxious children relax and get on with the business of having fun and learning.

Key points

- Anxiety is normal at different stages of development, and at certain points in a child's life (such as starting school, leaving home for the first time, or changing carers).
- Many symptoms of anxiety go unnoticed because children become adept at covering up the problem.
- Setting up regular routines, encouraging teamwork, teaching children to express their emotions and gently offering opportunities for independence will help children to overcome their anxiety.
- Remember that poor self-esteem can often be at the root of anxiety and fear. It does not take much to raise a child's self-image and encourage self-belief.

Chapter 5

Biting

Most parents and carers have to deal with biting in children – and even a biting epidemic – at least once in their careers. Many are, unsurprisingly, unsure of how to deal with it.

There is an amazing and surprising wealth of research into biting, but most of it points to the same thing. Biting is a normal developmental phase for infants and toddlers, with virtually no long-lasting developmental significance. Once a child turns three years old, however, biting may indicate other behavioural problems, especially if the biting incidents are frequent. But working out the cause of the biting can be fairly straightforward, and the problem easily addressed with a little perseverance.

Why do children bite?

Babies

Developmental theorists suggest that biting is probably a form of exploration – infants use their mouths to explore because it is one of the most developed parts of their bodies. Biting in infants may also be a primitive form of communication; it is likely that the infant does not connect biting to pain experienced by others. Babies also tend to be impulsive and lack control. Some babies may bite simply because something is there to bite; others bite when they are excited or over-stimulated. Teething pain may also be a precursor – as is a little natural experimentation with cause and effect.

Toddlers

Experts believe that biting in toddlers between 12 and 36 months old is a form of communication (ie. to communicate frustration while learning social, language, and self-control skills). There is also pretty clear evidence that toddlers seldom plan ahead, but that they see and act on what they are experiencing at the moment. They do not have the language necessary to control a situation, or their attempts at communication are not understood or respected. Biting becomes a powerful way to communicate with and control others and the environment. It is a quick way to get a toy or attention.

Many toddlers display extreme ranges of emotions, both happy and sad, and lack labels for communicating these emotions. Too many challenges (from activities that are too difficult), demands, wants, and obstacles can anger and frustrate toddlers and may lead to biting.

Many toddlers do not yet understand sharing or that touch can hurt, and they need to learn other ways to communicate besides biting. Research also shows that carers found that toddlers may also bite when they experience a stressful event, a particularly distressing lack of routine or inadequate adult interaction.

Research undertaken in 1995 found that toddlers may be more apt to bite if they have not interacted with adults for more than five minutes. Other toddlers may bite as a self-defence strategy or they may simply be imitating other toddlers who bite.

Pre-schoolers

Occasional or rare biting from pre-schoolers may occur for some of the same reasons as it does for infants and toddlers – to exert control over a situation, for attention, as a self-defence strategy, or out of extreme frustration and anger. Frequent biting after a child turns three, however, may indicate other behaviour problems, because by that time the majority of children have the communication skills necessary to relate their needs without biting.

A 1992 study put forward the idea that biting may also be caused by sensory integration dysfunction in a small number of young children. These children may respond negatively to touch sensations, becoming anxious, hostile or aggressive. They may be under- or over-responsive to touch, or react negatively when others are close. Light touches from behind may be particularly distressing, leading, in some situations, to biting.

Types of biters

Why young children bite can help you deter this aggressive behaviour and teach them positive ways to handle their feelings. Researchers have broken biters down into the following categories:

The experimental biter

An infant or young child may take an experimental bite out of a mother's breast or a caregiver's shoulder. These experimental biters may simply want to touch, smell and taste other people in order to learn more about their world. Their muscles are developing, and they need to experiment. This type of biter may also be motivated by teething pain.

The frustrated biter

Some biters lack the skills to cope with situations, such as the need for an adult's attention or another child's toy. Even though the child may not have intended to harm another person, adults must react with disapproval.

The threatened biter

Some children, feeling they are endangered, bite in self-defence. They may feel overwhelmed by their surroundings and bite as a means of regaining control. Children may become threatened by situations such as newly-separated parents, the death of a family member, or a mother returning to work. The threatened biter may require additional nurturing, particularly if the danger has to do with something more serious, such as physical violence at home.

The power biter

Some children experience a strong need for autonomy and control. As soon as they see the response they get from biting, the behaviour is strongly reinforced.

What to do

Young children may bite for different reasons, and not all will respond to the same types of intervention. Identifying the kind of biter you are dealing with (see above) will help you develop an appropriate discipline technique.

- When a baby or experimental biter bites, adults should use prompt, clear signals to communicate that children must not bite people. 'No,' said sharply, would be an appropriate response.
- Infants may not yet understand the difference between biting a toy and biting a person, so a repeated message in an honest tone of voice that conveys pain (saying: 'Ouch, that hurt me!') can help teach babies aged four months and older not to bite others.
- Provide them with a variety of surfaces to play on and a colourful selection of toys to stimulate children during this stage of exploration.
- If teething is a cause, offer children appropriate things to chew on for relief: Very cold, large carrots, teething biscuits, or a safe teething ring.
- If a child bites out of frustration, tend to the victim immediately. Then explain to the biter that biting hurts others and is not allowed.
- You may help frustrated biters by teaching them appropriate language to show their feelings or get what they need. Give positive reinforcement when children communicate effectively. Also, watch for signs of rising frustration. Spotting potential conflict may help you intercept a potentially harmful incident.
- In the case of a threatened biter, use the intervention techniques already mentioned and reassure the child that his rights and possessions are safe. You may need to give extra attention and nurturing to make your bond as strong and nurturing as possible. A little t.l.c. may go a long way.
- Give a 'power' biter choices throughout the day, to satisfy his clear need for control, and reinforce positive social behaviour (like sharing and saying 'thank you'). If the biter gets attention when he is not biting, he will not have to resort to aggressive behaviour to feel a sense of personal power.
- Never hit or bite back a child for biting. This communicates that violence is an ppropriate way to handle emotion. The approach should be calm and educational. A child should not experience any reward for biting - not even the reward of negative attention.
- Two studies performed in the 1990s suggest that biters who have reached the age of two or older may benefit from assisting in the first aid process. The biter can assist the victim by demonstrating gentle touching, having the biter rub the victim's arm, and generally assisting with taking care of the victim to teach nurturing behaviour (without letting these activities become a game).
- Other sources recommend that biters should be removed from the situation without dramatic movements, attention, or an emotional response that could provide negative reinforcement to the biter.
- Stress communication skills. A 1995 study suggests that emphasis be placed on teaching biters to develop and use their expressive communication skills instead of biting, so they can learn to use words to express their feelings. Good caregivers consistently promote

the child's use of language to enhance cognitive development, and some experts believe that promoting children's language development is also helpful in reducing biting behaviours. For example, if another child is taking a toy away from a child who has a history of biting, caregivers can teach the potential biter to say 'stop', 'mine', etc., and tell the child: 'We do not bite people, we bite food,' or, 'It hurts when you bite.'

- Across various studies, other researchers suggest that using positive language to tell the child to touch gently rather than not to hit or bite can be helpful.
- They also suggest that caregivers can help children verbalise their feelings by saying: 'You look angry, Peter. Tell Amy to stop pulling, you do not like that.' Caregivers and parents should try to be specific with their language. Instead of saying: 'Stop being unkind to Peter,' for example, they can say: 'Peter is angry because you are taking his truck.'
- Some experts recommend consistently teaching the child to say: 'No,' to other children rather than biting.
- Some psychologists also recommend that efforts be made to examine the pattern of biting incidents to determine if factors such as crowding, over-stimulation, lack of toys, lack of attention or supervision, or other factors seem to precede biting episodes. On the basis of a 1999 study, Garcia suggests that caregivers become adept at observing the child's physical state and noticing whether factors such as new teeth, or other kinds of pain on a given day, seem to be associated with increased biting episodes.
- Caregivers might think about whether children bite when their bowels are irregular, when they are hungry or when they are sleepy. Some experts (including Garcia, above) believe that emotions and stress inducers such as a new baby in the house may also be associated with an increase in biting episodes for individual children.
- Be aware of the child's favourite toys and educational materials and duplicate these, because sharing is not always in the toddler's behavioural repertoire.
- Provide a variety of options and motor-sensory choices (eg. make the toys and climbing structures challenging but not so frustrating that the children become angry or bored). Adjust the schedule so that the children eat and nap when they are beginning to get hungry and tired rather when these conditions become extreme.
- Find ways to strengthen the sense of security and stability in the environment.
- Maintain a consistent routine that minimizes surprises for children.
- Ensure prime times with the child's favourite primary caregiver.
- Create warm, cosy places to be.
- Avoid unnecessary staffing changes.
- Develop and maintain group rituals.
- Researchers Claffey, Kucharski, and Gratz detail other environmental factors to consider, such as creating a balance of open and closed spaces in a home or nursery environment so the children may move about freely and yet feel protected but not overwhelmed.
- Take the time to look for patterns in the biter's environment and emotional state at each episode. Does the child always bite the same individual? Is the biter simply exhausted, or hungry? Be ready to intervene immediately, but carefully.

Chapter 5: Biting

In summary

Always look at the context in which a child bites and try to work out the motivation – is it teething? A need for power? Or simply an attention-seeking mechanism? Be aware of age-specific biting – a baby doesn't bite out of spite, and a five-year-old is unlikely to be exploring his environment. Act promptly and with patience, while teaching children better ways to deal with frustration and anger, such as verbalising their emotions. Most importantly, do not turn an isolated incident into a major event. Use it as an opportunity to teach children why biting is inappropriate behaviour.

Key points

- Children bite for different reasons at different ages – in babies, biting is usually experimental.
- Biting is only considered to be a problem after the age of three, when children should have the emotional capacity to learn and use different behaviours.
- Always react promptly but calmly to a biting incident, and take the opportunity to teach the biter why it is wrong.
- Try to assess motivation before choosing a discipline technique. Reacting harshly to a child who needs a little nurturing and attention will only compound the problem.
- Stress communication skills above all else, to encourage children to express themselves in ways that are not violent.

Chapter 6

Cheeky behaviour

Talking back and exhibiting cheeky behaviour is a normal part of development for pre-schoolers. However, if it is left unchecked it can lead to discipline problems in the future, which can affect a child's potential in the classroom and his ability to exercise self-control. Cheeky children can often be amusing in small doses but it is important, from an early age, to teach respect and the basics of courteous negotiation.

Talking back can be quite unsettling, particularly when children use angry or inappropriate language. We'll look at this whole issue a little later in the book (see page 149), but it does form a part of being cheeky, and needs addressing as a part of that syndrome. Many children play up in the company of their peers, largely because this type of behaviour is guaranteed to raise laughter; others respond in this manner because they have never been taught differently. In other words, parents or carers have responded to cheeky behaviour and back-talk by giving in, which has taught a child that he can achieve what he wants by being rude.

Only a couple of generations ago, the vast majority of children would not have dreamt of exhibiting the type of verbal insolence that so many children assume as a matter of habit today. Not surprisingly, parents, teachers and carers are bewildered by this increasingly cheeky attitude.

Why do children talk back?

- Discipline is the number one reason, according to the most recent research, undertaken in 2005 in the US. Parents of generations past did not tolerate back-talk in any way; if a child was mouthy, he was punished immediately. The new emphasis on self-esteem has given children freer rein to express opinions, even at a very young age, but how they express them is obviously the source of much controversy.
- Parents today also tend to give in to disrespectful demands, and respond to talking back and cheekiness with intermittent reinforcement, which means that children soon twig that this method of attaining what they want works.
- It is important to remember that during the early pre-school years, children's language skills are rapidly growing and they begin to recognise the impact of their own words. When words elicit a strong response from others, this can be a powerful experience for a young child. So if cheekiness gains them an instant, even explosive response, chances are they will continue.
- While young children are able to experience a wide range of emotions, they do not typically have the advanced language skills to fully express their feelings verbally. Back-talk, at this age, may be a child's attempt to verbalise some of the very powerful feelings that he is experiencing. Young children have not mastered the subtle nuances of language. 'I hate you' to a four-year-old, may actually mean, 'I was having fun and I didn't want to stop playing.'

- Children also tend to be heavily influenced by the media, in particular television, where sharp retorts, 'funny' comments and back-chat to authority figures are met with laughter. It is not surprising that they emulate what they see.
- Similarly, children mimic their parents and carers. Arguing on the telephone or with a partner or colleague, offering a rude retort to another driver, or even answering children's requests with a flippant reply, leads children to believe that this is a normal form of interaction.

A new study published in the October 2002 issue of the Journal of Child Psychology and Psychiatry suggests that three- and four-year-olds who have trouble recognising different emotions may be more likely than their more perceptive peers to behave aggressively once they start school. According to researchers, the results show that the connections between emotional understanding and behavioural problems begin early in a child's development.

There are other reasons, too, why some children are cheekier than others. Children with low self-esteem may elicit much-needed attention by constantly engaging a parent or carer in arguments or negotiation, by continually talking back or being disrespectful or defiant. Similarly, studies show that children who are depressed, have been bullied or abused, or under-parented tend to attract attention to themselves by talking back and rebelling.

Consider, too, the possibility that a child has learning difficulties. These make it difficult for the child to understand and take part in even basic classes, such as gym and music, and when they reach playgroup or reception classes, they may become bored, feel stupid and misbehave.

It is easier to be the class clown than it is to accept that you are somehow inferior or less able to keep up with the others. And do not dismiss age – even toddlers become frustrated if their efforts do not gain rewards, and they may develop habits that will make it difficult for them to succeed later on.

Finally, hyperactivity or hearing problems can also cause a child to be cheeky and a little wild – if children do not stop to catch the gist of what is going on, or they cannot hear properly, they may cover it up by acting up.

Does it matter?

Some children carry on behaving badly for several months or longer. Again and again they are disobedient and cheeky. Their behaviour escalates and, if unchecked, can begin to seriously break rules accepted within the classroom or family. And, of course, once one set of rules is overturned, it is easy to continue.

This sort of behaviour will affect a child's development and interfere with his ability to lead a normal life. When behaviour is this much of a problem, it is called a conduct disorder. About half of the young children who suffer from conduct disorder do improve over the years. However, half get worse.

Older children often develop a hostile, aggressive attitude as well as being disobedient and defiant. Later on, this kind of behaviour puts a huge strain on the family. Outside the home, children who behave like this will often find it difficult to make friends. Other children often do not want to know them because they are rude and cannot play without getting aggressive. Even though they might be quite bright, they do not do well at school and are often near the bottom of the class. They may cause trouble in lessons and be asked to leave.

Other people just see a violent, troublesome, irritating youngster. Inside, the young person may feel that they are worthless and that they just cannot do anything right. They often blame others for their difficulties and do not know how to change for the better.

This all may sound rather dramatic for a toddler or pre-schooler, but it is very important to remember that unacceptable behaviour that starts as a method of seeking attention, or in response to inadequate discipline or self-esteem, does become habitual. Children are easily labelled as difficult or cheeky – and labels are hard to shift. What is more, children are never given the opportunity to understand the impact of their behaviour, and if reducing a teacher or a carer to tears or fury gets them what they want, they will continue.

What can you do?

- Offer plenty of attention for good behaviour, and play down the 'bad', particularly if it is designed to provoke a response. It is all too easy to ignore children when they are behaving well, and only pay attention when they are behaving badly. Over time, children learn that they only get attention when they break the rules. Not surprisingly, even youngsters seem to prefer angry or critical attention to being ignored.
- Set firm rules. Whether you are a teacher, carer or parent, there should be golden rules (the equivalent of house rules) which should not be broken. Preset penalties should be set in place for transgressions, and they should be firmly implemented each and every time that rules are broken. Children need to learn that rules are important and that 'no' means 'no'.
- This does not mean that negotiation cannot be encouraged. There is nothing wrong with a child putting forward his point of view or expressing a disagreement, but the manner in which this objection is put forward is extremely important. Cheeky, rude behaviour should never be rewarded. However, listening to a reasonable argument, explaining your own reasons for saying no, and adjusting your stance in the face of a polite request, can certainly be encouraged. Indeed, other children will see that being polite, and requesting things without being rude, argumentative or cheeky, can reap rewards.
- Be consistent. Although there is no doubt that children can be wearing, giving in once is a tantalising lesson for a child to learn. Dogged determination is undoubtedly a normal quality in any pre-schooler and, if you give an inch, expect them to run the whole way with it.
- Remember that children do not necessarily know what is right and wrong, or what is acceptable. If you do not explain the reasons why talking back is rude and offensive, why being cheeky is hurtful and disruptive, and how consistently behaving in this way makes people unhappy, you cannot expect children to understand. Caring for children involves taking the time to spell things out, and making clear where the rules start and stop.

- Teach other means of getting opinions across. If a child talks back, calmly suggest that they re-phrase or use different words or a different tone of voice. Listen to them when they do this. If they struggle, give them the words: 'I am sure you are unhappy that Susie has the toy first and think it's unfair. Is that what you mean?'

Emotional literacy

It is clear that teaching empathy can go a long way towards encouraging the type of behaviour you want to see. Young children are just beginning to learn about their own feelings. It is a huge leap to learn that other people have feelings too. But it is important for children to begin the process of developing empathy, which means to know and care about other people's feelings, at an early age.

- Be attentive and respond to children's emotions. When you pay attention to children's emotions, they experience empathy first hand, from the beginning.
- Label your children's feelings. Say, 'It's nice to see you so happy', during good periods, or, 'Oh that's so frustrating' when a child is frazzled by a puzzle and beginning to lose it.
- Label your own feelings – 'I feel angry and sad when you speak to me like that.'
- Validate feelings. As in: 'I can see why you're angry. You wanted to keep playing, but now it's time for a nap'. This shows that you can see the world from the child's eyes.
- Stop aggressive behaviour and let a child know how you feel about it. When a child hits another child say 'You can't do that. You're hurting Susie.' Young children may not yet understand how others feel when they are hit, pushed or shoved, but they do understand when parents or carers, or anyone in authority, strongly disapprove of their behaviour – and they can begin to see that the disapproval is linked to their hurtful behaviour toward others.
- Teach a child to see things through other people's eyes. When a child hits someone, say: 'How do you think Susie feels when you hit her?' or 'How would you feel if Susan, or someone else, hit you?'
- Care for victims. When a child is hurt by another child, immediately stop the aggressive behaviour and attend to the victim. This shows caring and concern and also shows the aggressor that his behaviour is not directing your attention where he wanted it.
- Teach through play. Playing with dolls is a great way for girls and boys to learn about caring for others. Caring for others can also be taught and encouraged in the context of many types of imaginary and expressive play, such as artwork or puppetry.

Backchat is undoubtedly one of the first things a child does when he exerts his independence, and while you should welcome a point of view and encourage the art of negotiation, it is extremely important to teach children the skills necessary for polite interaction. Teach children to consider their words, and the impact that they have. Keep discipline firmly in place, but do not assume that children will automatically know the rules. Children need to have them explained, and your expectations made clear. With consistent use of discipline, rewards for good behaviour, and no-tolerance policies for rude back-chat, children will soon get the message. That does not mean stamping the humour or the personality out of a child.

Cheeky can undoubtedly be funny from time to time, but within acceptable boundaries. Give them the appropriate response to their behaviour, and teach them to understand how others feel when they are rude. Within the safe boundaries of good discipline, they will thrive and find their own personalities. Most importantly, however, they will develop self-respect and respect for others.

Key points

- Children who grow up without empathy for others are more likely to be rude, cheeky or to talk back.
- Teaching empathy is one of the key tools for parents and carers in ensuring courtesy and respect.
- Do not under-estimate the importance of self-esteem. Many outrageously cheeky children simply need attention, and use the only means they have at their disposal to obtain it.
- Be firm and consistent about discipline, and ask a child to re-phrase if they wish to dispute a point. However, make it clear that 'no' means 'no', and there are some occasions where arguments will not be considered – in issues of safety, for example.
- Cut down on teeny-bopper TV, which encourages children to be cheeky to authority figures. If the child's favourite show has a cheeky character, sit down and explain why it is not nice to behave like that in real life.

Chapter 7

Childhood fears

Fears are a normal part of childhood, and are an innate, protective response to situations or objects which are potentially threatening or dangerous. They change as children grow older, and are able to rationalise and cope with different situations or threats; however, they can be overwhelming and, in the extreme, affect a child's development. It's important to understand which fears are considered normal, and how they can be dealt with effectively so that a child can overcome them, and become secure and confident.

Consider a child's world – from babyhood it is a constant journey through uncharted waters. He moves from his mother's arms to explore his immediate surroundings, and into the big, wide world. Every day he pushes at the boundaries of what is safe and familiar.

Some children are naturally more curious and robust, taking new encounters into their strides. Others are more cautious, and lack the confidence to deal with new situations without help. From a child's viewpoint, there are many wonders – and dangers: steps, roads, dogs, fires, darkness, unfamiliar adults, loud noises and electrical sockets. As they grow up children learn how to deal with these fears and then how not to be afraid of them. This learning process continues through childhood, with each new experience teaching the child more about the world, and reducing his fear of the unfamiliar and threatening.

It is important to note that fears are only abnormal if they are persistent or keep a child overly preoccupied with the feared object or subject, so that it interferes with normal activities, if a child cannot be reassured or distracted away from the fear (becoming a phobia), or if it is an irrational fear. Whether or not a fear is irrational depends on a child's age and developmental level. For example, it is normal for a toddler to fear having a bowel movement on the toilet, but it would be irrational for a six-year-old to have the same fear.

Types of fears

The main types of fears which affect children are: environmental, imaginary and social. Environmental fears are understandable anxieties about real things such as animals, thunder, the dark and burglars. Imaginary fears are worries about things such as ghosts and monsters from stories and films. Social fears are anxieties about social situations such as being separated from a parent, being left at nursery, starting school, and joining a sports or some other group for the first time.

These three groups tend to follow a roughly chronological order, with toddlers and pre-schoolers more prone to environmental fears, older pre-schoolers and early primary school children more likely to experience imaginary fears and social fears persisting through to the teenage years and beyond.

Chapter 7: Childhood Fears

Toddlers and pre-schoolers normally have simple fears of separation, noises, falling, animals and insects, using the potty or toilet, bathing and bedtime. They may also develop a fear after a triggering event, such as falling in the water or touching something hot. Fears may also increase during times of stress (for example a new baby, moving or divorce).

Some children are more fearful of things, even common things, than others and this is usually according to their type of temperament. Also, parents who are very anxious or fearful, or who tend to over-react to things, often have children who have the same reactions in similar situations.

Dealing with fears

1. Prepare your child

When a child is prepared for an experience that he might consider frightening, he will be better equipped psychologically to deal with it. For example, a child going to school for the first time will need to know that mum or carer will be leaving him there; that a lightning bolt may be followed by a very loud noise called thunder; that there will be strangers at the birthday party he is attending, or there are likely to be spiders under the bed when you do the spring cleaning. Provide as much information as possible about what is going to happen in any situation. There is no doubt that knowledge inoculates against fear.

2. Be a good role model

Show a child how to respond to a potentially frightening situation through your own behaviour. This helps in several ways. First, it shows a child what to do in a situation, which increases confidence and empowers a child. Second, it shows him that nothing bad is going to happen to him. Third, it teaches him the lesson that even if you are feeling a bit frightened, facing a fear is the best way to deal with it. It is extremely important to keep your own anxieties under wraps. On a personal note, I once had an au pair who was absolutely terrified of spiders and would scream the house down if one appeared. My two boys, aged three and five, soon developed an irrational fear of creepy-crawlies which took years to overcome. Never underestimate the effect of an over-reaction. Children can be taught to be afraid of things, which they would otherwise happily deal with, by observing others' anxieties.

3. Little by little

If a child has a particular fear, help him to overcome it by exposing him to it in gradual steps, from least to most frightening. For example, if he is afraid of dogs, start with pictures of dogs, then observe dogs at a distance, then pat a small, quiet dog, then pat and stroke bigger, passive dogs. If he is afraid of a monster under the bed or in the cupboard, draw pictures of nice monsters (Sesame Street springs to mind), have a good clear-out of the cupboard, discuss the idea that monsters are really only imaginary, puppets or cartoons, and encourage him to confirm to you that monsters are not in the cupboard or anywhere else in the house.

Graduated exposure to the feared object or situation is more likely to be successful than making a child leap straight into a situation which runs the risk of increasing his anxiety about it. Let a child set the pace by choosing what the next step will be in confronting his fear. Progress will be more rapid if he stays within his comfort zone as he moves from step to step.

4. Reinforcement with praise

Highlight and praise the progress a child is making in dealing with his fears. Reinforce the message that he is being very brave, because in doing so you are making the quality of being brave a part of his self-image, which will help him to deal with future fears. If he believes that, he'll be more likely to become it.

Naturally fearful children

A small percentage of children seem to be fearful by nature or temperament. From an early age their usual response to new situations tends to be avoidance or withdrawal, and they seem to be generally more worried and anxious than other children. Parents, teachers and carers can often become exasperated and frustrated with anxieties and clinginess, a reaction which makes the problem worse.

In this case, it's worth considering the following:

- Accept that a child has a genuine problem and is not just being difficult for the sake of it.
- Adjust expectations to a level matching the child's perceptions.
- Find the delicate balance between encouraging and supporting a child to try new activities without placing them under the constant pressure of being forced to do things that don't come naturally.
- Don't hesitate to get some professional help from a child psychologist if a child's enjoyment of life is being significantly impaired by the severity of his anxieties.

Dealing with fears in general

- Respect a child's feelings and fears. It is not helpful to use put-downs, such as 'Don't be such a baby', or to try to ignore the things that he is afraid of. Fears are real and they must be acknowledged for a child to deal with them.
- Ask him why he is afraid and then talk about it. This can be especially helpful if there was a triggering event.
- Don't be over-protective and do encourage a child to avoid all the things that he is afraid of. He'll never learn the coping mechanisms necessary to deal with this fear, or others in the future. Similarly, however, do not force a child to do something he is afraid to do. Use the four-step plan to gradually work your way towards acceptance.
- Don't overreact – extra attention reinforces a child's reactions.
- Set up a firm routine – at home, in the classroom, whatever you are doing with a child. Children thrive on routine and know what to expect next, which makes them feel more secure and able to deal with new challenges.
- Use books to open up conversation and to show different ways of coping in different

situations and with different fears. *The Owl Who Was Afraid of the Dark* (Jill Tomlinson and Paul Howard) or *When I Feel Afraid* (Cheri J Meiners and Meredith Johnson) are good examples.

- Use artwork and puppets, or even television programmes, as starting points. Encourage a child to express fears, and come up with amazing solutions for dealing with them.
- Give a child support as he learns to master his fears. For example, if a child is afraid of starting a new school, be empathetic and understanding. Give the fear a name, so that the child is better able to verbalise what he is feeling. But remain positive, and point out how the fear can be overcome. For example, 'You might be worried about making new friends, or leaving behind mum or carer, and it's OK to feel a bit frightened. The good thing is that you will feel better very soon.' Ask him how he feels and what makes him feel happy. If he is shy about meeting new children, introduce him to some situations where he will meet others on his own terms.
- Remind him of other things or times in the past that he was afraid of, and for which he no longer has fears.
- Teach the child how to rate fear. If your child can visualise the intensity of the fear on a scale of one to 10, with 10 being the strongest, he may be able to see the fear as less intense than first imagined. Younger children can think about how full of fear they are, with being full 'up to my knees' as not so scared, 'up to my tummy' as more frightened and 'up to my head' as truly petrified.

When fears become phobias

When anxieties and fears persist, problems can arise. Sometimes, despite the best efforts of parents, teachers and carers, children do not grow out of anxieties and their causes loom larger and become more prevalent. The anxiety becomes a phobia, or a fear that is extreme, severe and persistent. A phobia can be very difficult to tolerate, both for the child and those around him, especially if the anxiety-producing stimulus is hard to avoid. But the good news is that unless a child's phobia hinders his everyday ability to function, he will rarely need treatment by a professional because in time the phobia will be resolved.

It's important, however, for parents and carers to keep tabs on fears. A few general questions, checked frequently, can help you to do just that. For example, what are the symptoms of the fear? How do they affect the child's personal, social and academic functioning? If symptoms can be identified and considered in light of the child's everyday activities, adjustments can be made to alleviate some of the stress factors. If you don't recognise the problem, easy solutions cannot be undertaken, such as helping a child who is afraid of the dark feel more comfortable about falling asleep in a darkened room. Often small interventions, undertaken early, can nip a fear in the bud.

Does the fear seem unreasonable in relation to the reality of the situation? Could it be a sign of a more serious problem? If the child's fear seems out of proportion to the cause of the stress, this may signal the need to seek outside help, such as a counsellor, psychiatrist or psychologist. Look for patterns. If an isolated incident is resolved, don't make it more significant than it is. But if a pattern that is persistent or pervasive emerges, then you really do need to intervene, or the phobia will impact on a child over time. Your child's doctor can be consulted, as can a mental health professional who has expertise in working with children.

All children experience fears as a normal part of development, and they should be encouraged to understand what they are feeling and to develop coping mechanisms. Never under-estimate the effect of fear which can, if left unchecked, develop into a phobia. While it is important to address fears gradually, pushing a fearful child can have the opposite effect and lead to terror. A firm routine and lots of support and guidance will help a child get over even the most entrenched fears, and help him to develop the security and confidence he needs to deal with difficult situations and frightening experiences in the future.

Key points

- All children experience fears, and these differ as they grow older.
- There are three main types of fears; imaginary, environmental and social, all of which will be experienced to some extent by all children.
- Children with a strong, secure routine, who are given coping skills as a part of everyday life, feel more secure and able to deal with new challenges and frightening situations.
- Some children are more 'constitutionally fearful', and will require a little extra help to overcome their shyness or fearfulness.
- Left unchecked, a fear can become a phobia, so it's important for carers and parents to nip problems in the bud as early as possible, and this means watching out for symptoms and then acting upon them.

Chapter 8

Clingy Children

A clingy child can be difficult for parents, carers and teachers alike, as activities often have to be curtailed, and extra, time-consuming attention offered, often at busy moments.

All children are clingy at some point in their childhood, and almost all babies experience some form of separation anxiety, which is one of the greatest causes of clingy behaviour. However, as children get older, their tendency towards clinginess often reflects stress, anxiety, fear or insecurity. These can be short-term problems and some children need special care to instil independence and security, in order to avoid remaining shy or sensitive well into their teenage years and even adulthood.

Separation anxiety usually becomes evident in children at about six months of age. At this stage, most infants have developed a very strong attachment to their primary caregivers. This strong attachment leads to a feeling of great distress when the primary caregiver and the child must be separated. Separation anxiety can continue off and on, though usually in milder forms, throughout childhood. It can be quite intense during infancy, with this intensity gradually decreasing as children get older and become more and more accustomed to being separated from their primary caregivers. It is normal for children to feel some sort of distress or upset when separated from parents, especially separations for long periods of time.

Separation anxiety can take many forms; many young infants will protest when their mothers simply leave the room for a minute or two – they have difficulty with even the shortest of separations. Older children may be just fine playing by themselves, but then experience difficulty, for example, when their parents go out for an evening, leaving them at home with a sitter. At first, separations are often very difficult for both children and their primary caregivers, but as parents and their children become accustomed to being apart, the process usually becomes easier.

While separations are often difficult for both parents and their children, children who are raised in families in which both parents work outside the home tend to have less difficulty with separations because they begin experiencing them at a very young age. Therefore, children who are older when they face their first separations from their primary caregivers often have a more difficult time making the adjustment.

Stress

As we shall discuss further, stress is more common in pre-schoolers than previously believed, and one of its most common manifestations is clinginess – to parents, caregivers, teachers and anyone who appears to offer security and comfort. Common causes of stress include changes in household arrangements or carers and family divorce. Children aged two, three or even younger are very sensitive to family tension. The death of a family member, friend or pet can also cause a great deal of anxiety, as can the birth of a sibling.

The way a child reacts to stress depends a great deal on his age, experiences and personality. Resilience, which protects children from stress, is mainly linked to a child's personality. What proves stressful for one child might not be for another. In general, children who are positive and deal head-on with problems rather than letting them mount up will be less stressed and better able to cope.

Fears

You will remember that there are three main types of fears: environmental, imaginary and social, and that these three groups tend to follow a rough chronological order.

Temperament

Many school-age children experience uncomfortable, anxious feelings when they are away from their parents. Every child is born with more or less of a tendency to feel anxious. Children who are very sensitive are often more prone to anxiety and worry than their less sensitive peers. Parents don't create this tendency toward anxiousness by anything they do or do not do. A child's natural temperament plays a big role. Often, only one child in a family will be prone to anxiousness, while the others are outgoing.

At the same time, parents who are empathetic to their children sometimes begin to think of a son or daughter as being particularly sensitive. The child, in turn, may live up to his parents' expectations, and act even more anxiously than he otherwise would. Not surprisingly, a more sensitive child will be that much more likely to cling. Parents, teachers and carers have to tread a fine line between being sensitive to a child's needs, and encouraging independence in a child who is simply living up to a label.

What to do

- Be open and honest with feelings. Children need an atmosphere where the open expression of feelings and questions is encouraged. Listen. Be affectionate. Warm hugs are reassuring and confirm to a child that you will be there when he needs you. A child who feels able to express himself, who is physically and emotionally loved, will feel good about himself, and develop a strong sense of self-worth and self-belief.
- Children often act out their fears and emotions of grief through high activity levels, the use of seemingly inappropriate humour, clinginess, withdrawal or aggressive behaviours. It's important to look at the cause of the fear and to deal with that rather than to clamp down on the behaviour.
- Make activities as routine as possible, so that a child understands what is happening and what comes next. Security is often enhanced by routines.
- Adults and children view family troubles in different ways. Adults generally have a

more complete understanding, more information and better coping skills. Children, on the other hand, usually don't fully grasp what's happening or why. And since they're naturally egocentric, they tend to believe everything is their fault. Parents, therefore, must make a conscious effort to reassure a child that troubles are not his fault.

- Don't go out of your way to avoid separations. It is part of life for children to learn to accept and deal with separation from their primary caregivers. Therefore, it is not a good idea for parents to try to avoid the pain of separation and stay with their children at all times. Instead, parents should go about their normal lives and separate when necessary, but at the same time they should make sure their children have consistent, quality care when they are not there.
- Introduce new caretakers (babysitters, for example) gradually. It is a good idea to allow your children to get to know their caretakers before being left alone with them.
- Provide transitional objects. Transitional objects are things that children often use to cope with separation. Such objects – for example, a teddy bear, a doll or a favourite blanket –give comfort to children when they are separated from their primary caregivers. Many children become attached to such objects, especially at times of separation (such as bedtime). Transitional objects can be quite a comfort to children experiencing some form of separation.
- Don't ignore a child's distress. The upset that children feel when they must be separated from their parents or carers is real. Therefore, this distress should not be shrugged off or ignored. Ignoring this distress can provoke more anxiety and will probably increase clinginess and distress. Instead, without making too big a deal out of it, address the upset.
- Certain separations are unavoidable; for example, when a mother must go to work and leave her child with a sitter. However, while at home, parents can try to accommodate a child who protests at being left alone by taking the child with them when they must leave the room that the child is in.
- Encourage children to do things for themselves. Parents and carers should begin teaching their children responsibility and independence while they are young. Children who are able to do some things for themselves are likely to see themselves as self-sufficient, and as a result will be less dependent upon their parents and less clingy.
- Prepare children for departures in advance. When parents or carers must leave their children, they should prepare them for this event beforehand so that they have time to get used to the idea. This information should be repeated periodically until you are sure that the child understands.
- Let a child know when you leave. Parents should never try to sneak out when they must leave their children. This can break down trust and increase clinginess. Children who are left in this way will be less apt to become absorbed in activities in the future because they will never know when they'll look up to find their parents gone.
- Let a child know when you plan to return. Parents and carers should make sure that their children know when they will return. If children are too young to tell time, you can mention time markers, such as 'after your nap', 'when you wake up' or 'after the Tweenies'.
- Many children need reassurance before and after separations. Parents and carers should provide lots of love and affection through both words and gestures (hugs, kisses) to

their children. Many children, when they must be separated from their parents or another important carer or loved one, may erroneously believe that they are being left in someone else's care because they are bad, or because their parents just don't want to be with them.
- Practise. Parents and carers should try to help their children get used to separations at an early age. For example, parents can try leaving the room for a couple of seconds at a time, and then reappearing. This will help young children learn that you will indeed return after you go away.
- Warmth and approval from one or a few consistent caregivers are the essential ingredients of trust – the basis for healthy emotional development.
- Remember that it's in the first two to three years of life that children's personalities are being most actively moulded – by the attitudes of the parents or of the others who provide most of their care. Give plenty of love, attention, affection and approval in order to help create a happy and emotionally secure child.
- Children gain trust in themselves from being respected as human beings by their parents or caregivers. This self-assurance helps them to be comfortable with themselves and with all kinds of people for the rest of their lives.

It's certainly possible to undo factors that may have caused a child to become anxious and clingy. Doing things to a routine, being open and accepting, and developing a child's sense of self-worth and trust will all help to alleviate the problem. Remember that some children are by nature more sensitive, and may need extra reassurance until they develop trust and a sense of independence.

The best way to deal with clinginess is to work out the causes, such as fears or stress, and address these first. Then focus on making a child's world a safe and loving place to be. Clinginess will then be a thing of the past.

Insecurity

Children whose sense of security is damaged can spend the rest of their lives in a desperate (often unaware) scramble to regain it. There are many situations that can shake or destroy a child's sense of safety:

- a child is made to feel responsible for family troubles.
- a divorce, death, physical or mental illness, or substance-abuse problem within the family.
- absent, inattentive, overly critical, cynical, and emotionally distant parents.
- volatile, violent or sexually abusive environment (for child, parent, sibling or friend).
- abandonment.
- parents hover over child or smother child.
- a child is forced to deny reality.
- a child suffers a traumatic event.
- parents love conditionally (child must behave in a certain way in order to be loved).

Chapter 8: Clingy Children

Insecure children need to feel safe in order to develop independence. It's important to remember that children depend upon adults for their self-image, identity and self-worth. They need to feel safe and unconditionally loved and valued; they need permission to be themselves and to be happy, no matter what is happening around them.

Key points

- All children will experience some separation anxiety, the level of which will be determined by how accustomed they are to separation at a young age. This type of anxiety is one of the greatest causes of clinginess.
- Children who are stressed or fearful will exhibit clinginess in an attempt to gain comfort and reassurance.
- Regular leave-taking, with plenty of reassurance, will help children to learn to trust.
- Some children are naturally more sensitive, and will require extra attention and regularity in their lives before they are able to let go and become more independent.

Chapter 9

Cry babies

Children may cry for many reasons, ranging from serious health problems to being hungry. Ignoring a baby's cry has now been shown to affect emotional development, including self-regulation. Even more worrying, perhaps, is the fact that excessive, uncontrolled crying that persists beyond three months of age has been linked with behavioural problems and lower IQ at the age of five. So is it normal for toddlers and pre-schoolers to cry? And what about those who seem to cry all the time, for the smallest of reasons, disrupting the routines of their household and childcare environments? The simple answer is that children in this age group should not feel the need to cry regularly, as it can indicate a host of different problems. Let's look at these now.

Why do children cry?

Crying is one way that humans express their emotions. It is one of the most effective ways a child who cannot speak communicates with others. Infants and young children cry for many reasons. As children mature into adults, crying occurs less often, and the reasons for crying become more specific. It is often not clear why children are crying. It is a caregiver's job to figure out why a child is crying and to relieve the underlying distress, if possible. Here are a few broad reasons why children who are past infancy cry:

Physical illness

Children cry when they are in pain from an injury or illness. Injuries are usually obvious. But the source of pain may not be so apparent in a child who cannot talk, or one who is younger than two or three. Ear infections are a common cause of pain in young children. These occur more often in the winter months and if a child has a nose or throat infection.

Toddlerhood

Toddlerhood, the time when children are between the ages of 12 and 36 months old, can be very frustrating for many young children. Toddlers have a strong need to assert their independence. This need to be independent, along with being stubborn and having a shortage of other options, leads toddlers into conflict with their parents and carers. This can result in the toddler being frustrated at not having his way. This frustration is expressed through crying and temper tantrums. Slowly, the toddler learns the rules, becomes more independent and develops his use of language. As his needs and feelings come to be expressed verbally, a young child uses crying less often to communicate.

Attention-seeking

Children sometimes use crying as a way to get an adult's attention. A child learns this if an adult attends to him every time he cries. After the first year of life, children can learn to comfort and quiet themselves when they go to bed and when they are not ill.

Some parents have adopted the ideology that children can comfort themselves when they are much younger, hence the success of the 'Contented Little Baby' series of books. Proponents claim that this teaches young children to be self-sufficient – they effectively learn not to cry. But at what expense?

The loss of emotional expression is one aspect which appears to affect the development of the parts of the brain that govern emotion. So a quieter baby may be the result, but by no means does that mean a more contented baby. Don't be tempted to believe the hype. No baby under the age of one is attention-seeking. Crying is the only real means of communication they have. But older children, say from 18 months onwards, can learn that crying is not a means of getting positive attention and feedback.

Irritability

Children cry more if they are irritable. However irritability, like crying, is merely a symptom of a problem. There are many reasons why a child may be irritable. He may not be getting enough sleep through a poor routine, a late bedtime or over-stimulation. The average child, up until the age of about four, needs a good twelve hours' sleep. If the doesn't get this all at night, he needs a nap. In fact, most toddlers require naps until the age of four to balance sleep needs.

Furthermore, children have television sets, electric games and personal computers in their bedrooms – even very young children. They are over-stimulated and spend time that should be spent sleeping, playing. Watch out, too, for the child who has a heavily orchestrated schedule – children who are involved in too many activities, with no time for quiet rest, reflection and unstructured play can actually experience stress, much like working adults. They become irritable, unable to relax and on a short fuse; hence the tears.

And don't rule out stress. Studies show that even babies can be stressed, by being left to cry, failing to have a sound, structured routine and through lack of sleep. An older child can be irritable if he is having problems at school, trouble with friends or if there is a lot of stress and tension in the home. Some children who live with a chronically irritable parent or carer can learn irritability as a way of life.

Depression

Children often do not exhibit the classic adult symptoms of depression. These include sadness, difficulty sleeping, appetite change or loss of motivation. Children who are depressed will be irritable, angry or fearful. They may cry or act up a lot. Younger children usually become depressed in response to significant, adverse changes in their social environment.

Other causes

Crying can become learned behaviour, just as not crying can. If a child sees a parent or carer crying in response to demands or frustration, he will learn this behaviour. If he learns that he always gets what he wants when he cries, he will use this as a tool to do so. A child who has low self-esteem or poor bonding with parents or carers, or who feels isolated or out of his depth (starting school before he is ready, for example) may also cry frequently, from frustration and may even display regressive behaviours (a common response to stressful situations).

What to do

- The first and most important thing is always to ensure that a child who cries frequently is not ill. Many illnesses are not apparent in a young child, who can not easily describe symptoms. He doesn't feel well and tears are the result. A chronic crier should always see a medical professional to rule out illness.
- Look, too, at routines and sleep patterns. Adults who are deprived of sleep feel fractious and tearful, so it's not surprising that children cry when they are overtired.
- A toddler's abilities to think and perceive are different from those of an adult, and they influence the way in which he will cope with adjusting to a new place. The toddler's world outlook is absolute. The infant mixes his self with the world, and only later does he distinguish between his private point of view and that of other individuals. The toddler believes that he is the centre of everything that takes place, and that things always remain as he sees them. Such patterns of perception make it difficult for the toddler to adjust to a new framework. He cannot understand why he must change his surroundings and move to a new place. He is focused on the things that he has found pleasure in and that have satisfied him so far, but now, with the move to a new framework, they are taken from him. This is important in terms of introducing a child to a new environment or to change of any sort, including new minders or a different routine. A young child will cry when he does not understand what is happening, and when events are out of his control. He will be unsure that his needs will be met, making him anxious.
- A strong routine is important to ensure that children get enough sleep, and it also helps them to feel more secure and calm enough to get to sleep. Even in the classroom or nursery, there should be routines that encourage quiet times, rest and relaxation, with stories, gentle music and quiet play.
- At bedtime or at naptime, it helps to put children over the age of 18 months in their own cots while they are still awake. This prevents them from thinking that they cannot go to sleep without an adult being with them.
- Remember that periods of crying will not harm a child. Young children should get enough affection, approval and attention during the daytime to meet their needs for feeling loved and accepted. They do not need reassurance of this in the middle of the night.
- Discourage a child from spending too much time on games consoles or computers or in front of the television. This can affect mood, lead to irritability and poor sleep and be the cause of countless battles.
- Avoid responding to crying that is directed at getting attention. Equally importantly, do not respond with anger or with punishment to the crying. This type of negative attention accomplishes the child's goal. Rather, say: 'Crying is not a good way to get my

attention. If you want me to spend time with you, please ask me in your normal voice.' If the child does not quickly respond, ignore the child and do something else.

- When the child has quieted himself, the adult should say something like: 'I'm proud that you were able to quieten yourself. It is much more fun to be with you when you are not crying. Now, what is it you wanted to do with me?'
- Set a good example. If you burst into tears when you are frustrated, your child, or any child you are caring for, will learn this behaviour. Express your frustration or another emotion in words, so that children learn that it is normal and acceptable to feel like crying in various circumstances, but that there are other ways of dealing with it, such as talking.
- Look at a child's schedule. If it is too busy, he'll be more likely to be stressed and overstretched. Ensure that there is plenty of down time for playing, creative activities and rest.
- Almost all children who are healthy and live in nurturing environments are happy and content most of the time. Chronic crying and irritability are not normal for a healthy child. A child who cries or is irritable most of the time should be seen by a healthcare provider. If the cause seems to be clearly related to issues in the child's social environment, attempts should be made to get to the root of these issues and correct them.
- Children often continue to cry as long as it seems to work for them. When it doesn't, they eventually stop. If they are upset about something, we want them to learn to handle their feelings in more powerful ways.
- One factor that generally triggers children to stop crying is social pressure. If older children cry often in front of peers, they will generally be ridiculed. Parents can point this out while they teach their children other, more powerful responses to difficult situations.
- It is important to encourage a child's sensitivity. We also want to teach both boys and girls to tolerate some feelings without crying and to express certain emotions in more mature ways.
- Don't isolate or reject a child for crying. This will exacerbate any feelings of anxiety.
- Don't try to talk a child out of crying by belittling his feelings. There is no point in saying 'there is no reason to cry' when the child clearly feels that there is. Explain that you understand the emotion causing the tears, and work on finding a solution to the problem – and a better way of dealing with it.
- Don't expect a child to immediately return to a happy, smiling state. Sadness, whether it is manufactured for attention or not, requires some time to dissolve.
- Remember that even when a young child seems determined to impose his will, he is also very eager to please adults. For this reason it's important to praise, praise, praise when he is frustrated, or when he does a good job at anything at all. This wish for approval is a carer's most reliable ally in the process of socialising the child. Appealing to it is far more effective and much healthier than threats of punishment.
- As they grow older, young children begin to feel shame along with wariness, or anxiety, and continue to develop emotions of fear, pleasure, pride and joy. It is not unusual for them to express anger and frustration by hitting, kicking, shoving or biting – and, of course, crying. Learning to recognise these emotions, connect them to their behaviour and to gain control over that behaviour is an ongoing process.

- Remember that a young child's cry is his way of trying to tell you something. Your response is an important way of saying back to the child: 'I hear you. I am trying to figure out what you want. You are important.' Research shows that consistently responding to infants is an important part of creating a strong, loving care-giving environment which supports the infant's development. This kind of continued responding is often referred to as responsive care-giving.
- Use books and creative play to talk about too much crying and the impact it can have on friendships, dealing with problems and overall happiness. Children need to and can easily learn that there are better ways to solve problems and communicate than crying. Good books to try include *Miffy Is Crying* by Dick Bruna and *Did You Think I Would Leave You Crying?* by Moira Miller.

Working out the cause of the crying, and ruling out ill-health are the most important ways to begin to deal with the problem. Look at sleep habits and even eating habits (a diet high in junk food can send blood sugar soaring and then plummeting, which can lead to tearfulness and irritability), as well as routine and scheduling. All children need quiet time, down time, quiet play and plenty of rest, along with positive stimulation. Too much of either can mean that sleep is disrupted, or moods affected. As a child grows older, much crying is in fact attention-seeking.

While it is important to acknowledge the emotion causing the crying, all children need to learn that crying is not a constructive way of dealing with problems or a way to get attention.

Key points

- Crying in a child under the age of 18 months should not be ignored, as social and emotional development can be affected.
- Rule out illness – both emotional and physical – as a cause of chronic crying.
- Don't give in to attention-seeking behaviour. Teach children that there are better ways both to get attention and to deal with problems.
- Ensure that strong routines are in place, particularly for a sensitive child who may be more prone to cry in periods of stress or change.
- Be a good role model – give a child a vocabulary to describe how he is feeling, the tools for solving problems, and then show that you use them both yourself.

Chapter 10

Daydreaming

Daydreaming, poor listening skills and lack of concentration can be frustrating for teachers and carers alike, but it is important to remember that there could be a good reason why children have their minds elsewhere. Let us look at the reasons why children 'wander', and the best ways to get them back on track.

Whether your daydreamer is sitting on the sofa or in the back row of your classroom, there is no doubt that it can be difficult to grab and keep his attention. Although some daydreaming is undoubtedly healthy – in fact, numerous studies have shown that daydreaming fosters a child's imagination, and enhances creativity – the danger is, of course, that a daydreaming child does not concentrate on his environment, and tends to shut himself away from reality. In some situations, such as near a busy road or in a swimming pool, this can be an accident waiting to happen.

Furthermore, children who have trouble concentrating and listening in a classroom environment can fall behind, and never quite grasp the basics of learning. Peer interaction also suffers and, at crucial stages of development, this can have a long-term impact.

Why will a child drift away?

Many health conditions can affect a child's ability to concentrate, and it is worth ruling these out if daydreaming and lack of concentration are a particular problem. It is always important to draw to a parent's attention any symptoms that you find worrying. Most health problems can be easily resolved. Similarly, if emotional issues are at the root of the problem, parents need to be advised that their child is experiencing difficulties.

Lack of sleep

In one American study, 26% of children who reported having inadequate sleep were found to nod off in 10-second micro sleeps in the classroom, losing concentration and finding it difficult to recover. Another study showed that children who get enough sleep demonstrate a better ability to concentrate, accomplish required tasks and handle minor irritations. By contrast, those with a higher 'sleep deficit' (regularly getting less than required) showed impairment of the ability to perform tasks involving memory, learning, logical reasoning and mathematical calculation. While it is difficult for teachers or carers to regulate sleep in their charges, it is worth mentioning your concerns to parents, and perhaps reading a story about sleep (*Can't You Sleep Little Bear?* by Martin Waddell is a good choice).

Hunger

Has the child had breakfast or a decent lunch? It may sound unlikely, but hungry children are less likely to interact with other people or explore or learn from their surroundings.

This interferes with their ability to learn from a very early age. School-aged children who are hungry cannot concentrate or do as well as others on the tasks they need to perform to learn the basics. What is more, anaemia can result from a poor diet. Although iron deficiency in adults can cause lethargy, irritability and a feeling of exhaustion, in childhood the symptoms of iron deficiency can be different. Some of the symptoms can include irritability, inability to concentrate, impaired cognitive skills, and shortened attention span.

Encourage children and parents to bring healthy snacks to school or, if you are looking after a child at home, make a good breakfast or regular snacks a part of your routine. It is also worth teaching children about the importance of eating well. A good book for story time is *Breakfast with the Bears*, by Patti Jennings and Poppy Wells.

Too much TV

This almost always plays a role in distracting a child from the mundane realities of life, and sets him off on a parallel tangent. While 'losing themselves' in a book or story can have the same effect on children, it does, however, offer a point of contact and the opportunity for interaction.

Lack of exercise

Very often the lack of a physical workout is compensated by an over-active 'mental workout'. Use breaks to do some physical activity, and ensure that you make the most of any organised sports or PE.

Learning disorders

ADHD and ADD children often find it difficult to concentrate and listen. There is a complex series of attributes for each of these disorders and it is worth familiarising yourself with them if you find that a child's attention span is noticeably poor.

Hearing problems

Hearing impairment can cause problems, such as lack of social skills, difficulty with communication and an inability to pay attention. When hearing loss is not diagnosed, it can appear that someone does not listen, misses details in a conversation or is not interested. Children with hearing loss can appear to be forgetful when they simply did not hear correctly. Children can become socially isolated and lack proper social skills to get along with their peers. If you suspect a hearing problem, mention this to the child's parents or carers as soon as possible.

A new situation

In some cases a child might not want to accept an unpleasant situation that he is faced with. This could be a constant stressful situation at home or school. The child then finds it easier, and certainly more fun, to mentally disappear into another more pleasant world of his own creation, a world of fantasy in which he can have whatever he likes, even things that he cannot have in reality.

In other cases the child is so obsessed with his own thoughts that he is absolutely unconcerned by the happenings in his environment. So even though he is physically present, he is mentally in absentia and loses sight and sound of everything around him.

Lack of interaction at home

Some withdrawn children have not developed effective conversational skills because their parents seldom converse with them or respond positively to their verbal initiations, and they have not had much opportunity to interact with peers. This circumstance may explain some of the shyness seen in nursery and reception classes.

School phobia

Children starting school for the first time may exhibit school phobia (usually fear of the unknown or unwillingness to be separated from the parent, rather than a specific negative reaction to the teacher or the school). Encourage children to talk about their fears, and help them to realise that everyone feels nervous from time to time. Again, books and discussions can help. *Rosie's First Day at School (Talking it Through)* by Rosemary Stones is a good first story.

Back on track

In a classroom or nursery environment:

- Seat daydreamers near you, and near the front of the activity. Gently and regularly include them in conversations or discussions.
- Display their (good) artwork or assignments for others to see in the classroom, to promote self-respect and encourage an interest in fulfilling assignments.
- In 1995, researcher Brophy surveyed effective teachers to find out how they responded to withdrawn students. The most commonly mentioned responses included:
  1. Changing the social environment (for example, seating them among friendly classmates or assigning them to a partner or small group).
  2. Encouraging or shaping increased responsiveness.
  3. Minimizing stress or embarrassment.
  4. Engaging shy students in special activities.
  5. Involving them in frequent private talks.

Conspicuously absent from these teachers' responses was emphasis of threat or punishment.

In 1998, researchers Blanco and Bogacki's recommendations from school psychologists for coping with general shyness withdrawal echo many of these same themes. They suggested involving them frequently in small-group, co-operative interaction with peers; using them as peer tutors; determining their peer preferences and seating them near preferred peers; leading but not forcing them to communicate; avoiding putting them in situations that would be embarrassing or frightening; and assigning them to messenger roles or other tasks that require communication.

For students whose withdrawal symptoms include excessive daydreaming, researchers suggest:

- calling on them frequently
- standing near them to ensure attention
- making sure that they get started successfully on their assignment at the beginning of work time, rather than scolding them for daydreaming
- stressing the need for attention and participation
- assigning partners to work with them and keep them involved.

Assign a daydreamer as a partner to, or promote their friendship with, a classmate who is popular and engages in frequent contact with peers. Ensure regular breaks. No child is able to concentrate for long stretches of time. No activity should run for longer than 30 minutes for children under the age of five or six. Physical activity breaks interspersed with time for creative endeavour can help to provide variety that will be stimulating.

Try to find out the particular interests, likes and dislikes of your daydreamer. If you can engage his attention by making topics relevant to his sphere, you are more likely to keep it. Make time to talk with the daydreamer each day, even if just for a few minutes. Listen carefully and respond specifically to what he tells you.

Do not hesitate to mention your concerns to parents or carers. It may well be that there is a health or other problem at the root, which can be dealt with by early intervention. Encourage parents to let you know when there is a family or other domestic problem. Many children who withdraw are simply escaping from problem situations. If you know the problems in advance, you can make a special effort to include a child or work through problems with appropriate information books (for example about divorce, shyness or new siblings).

At home:

- A regular routine with plenty of breaks for exercise, creative endeavours and relaxation will help to ensure that children are able to listen and concentrate when they need to.
- Offer regular snacks and, if appropriate, naps.
- If the child has homework, sit down and make a checklist with him. Make sure he completes his assignments, but encourage him to do this on his own.
- Watch television hours. No child will benefit from too much TV. Set out your expectations in advance, and turn off the television when agreed viewing is finished. Sit down with children when they watch TV and talk about what you are watching.
- Converse as frequently as possible with children, so that they become accustomed to regular interaction.

- Watch out for labels. If a child grows up believing that he is 'shy' or a 'daydreamer', he will be likely to retreat into that label and remain there.

Some children are undoubtedly distant as a feature of their personalities; others simply need to be encouraged out of their shells and into the present. First and foremost, however, it is important to work out if there is an external cause for this type of behaviour. Only then can it be addressed appropriately.

With a little patience, gentle nudging, increased responsibility and relevant interaction, even the most withdrawn children can and will sit up and take note.

Key points

- There may be a health problem causing poor attention and daydreaming. Mention your concerns to parents.
- Many children withdraw as a tool for dealing with difficult situations. See if you can find out what's making the child's life difficult.
- Offer plenty of reassurance and constant and regular interaction. Gently guide a withdrawn child back to reality with a series of questions.
- Ensure regular breaks, with time allowed for daydreaming. Make it clear, however, that concentration is required for other activities.
- Put a withdrawn child in charge of a group or activity, to boost confidence and engage attention.

Chapter 11

Faddy Eaters

Pre-school children often go through stages of faddy eating – a problem guaranteed to cause parents and carers concern and frustration, as they feel helpless to control and put into place healthy eating habits. Faddy eating is, however, a normal developmental stage in young children when they are beginning to assert their independence, and there are many reasons why the trend may continue for short periods as children grow older. What is important, however, is to adopt a sensible and calm approach to food and eating, to prevent a short-term issue from becoming a full-scale problem that affects a child's health and well-being.

It's very, very difficult to plan healthy, balanced meals when you are looking after children who refuse to eat them. Early in life, most children cotton on to the fact that their parents and carers are concerned about how much and what they are eating. Making a fuss about food guarantees instant attention; many children slide into the habit of using food to wield power over their carers.

Other children are simply not interested in food and the concerted efforts of their carers to make them eat put them off even further. The best advice is to remove the pressure. If children fail to get a response, they get bored. If they realise that they won't get attention for eating badly, they'll stop using food as a tool to do so. If the pressure is off at the dinner table, children will start developing a healthier attitude to food – that it's there to eat. It's neither poison nor is it a miracle medicine. Food can be enjoyed when it is not associated with parental nagging.

What causes food fads?

All children who are becoming independent will choose their own means to assert their authority. Mealtime is a perfect venue for a little rebellion: children have the full attention of their parents and carers, and they realise that food can provoke a fairly emotive response. So a natural inclination to exert independence often manifests itself at mealtimes.

In the first year of weaning, children grow a great deal and consume a lot of food – often without any fuss. When that growth slows down a little, after a child's second birthday, they are simply not as hungry. Many carers and parents are concerned that interest in, and intake of, food dwindles and they struggle to put in place healthier programmes. But this emphasis on eating well often backfires, as it makes children feel pressured, powerless and frustrated, particularly when they are genuinely not hungry. The result? They try to exert a little authority themselves, and the dinner table becomes a battleground.

One of the big issues, and cause for headline news these days, is the fact that children are simply not eating enough (and in some cases any) fruit and vegetables. According to the national diet and nutrition survey in the UK, which was published in 2000, 70% of pre-schoolers (between the ages of 18 months and four-and-a-half years) eat unhealthy foods such as biscuits, white bread, soft drinks, savoury snacks (including crisps and cereal-based snacks), chocolate, sweets and chips. Peas and carrots were the only cooked vegetables consumed by more than half the children and, of the vegetables, baked beans were consumed in the greatest quantities. Leafy green vegetables were eaten by only 39% of the children, and in fairly small quantities. And only 24% ate raw vegetables or salad. Some fruit appeared in the diets of most children, but it was limited mainly to apples, pears and bananas, while chocolate was consumed by 74% of children. Almost all had soft drinks (normally fizzy) and only a third of the children had fruit juice. Over 35% of their diets were made up of fats and 29% were sugars. So it's pretty clear that children are dictating what they eat – and winning out over parents' and carers' better judgement and concerted effort.

A recent independent survey conducted for children's vitamin manufacturer Haliborange discovered that two out of three children go through a stage of refusing to eat certain foods, and 65% of under-tens refuse fresh fruit and vegetables. Dr David Lewis, a psychologist who analysed the survey's results, advises parents to stop worrying: 'What seems like a food fad may simply be a part of growing up. Remember that tastes are highly individual and often take time to acquire. Keep in mind too that appetites change with age.'

Dr Lewis identifies six main food fads that young children might experience:

Anger fads.

By rejecting food the parents or carers have worked hard to prepare, a small child could be expressing anger or resentment he cannot put into words. He'll sulk, throw tantrums or become tearful. Food is not the real cause of this type of fad, so see if you can uncover what is really bothering the child.

Independence fads.

Refusing to eat certain foods, especially those that parents or carers want them to eat, makes a small child feel independent and grown up. This is very common around the age of four or five. The best way to address this one is to give children control in other areas of their lives (choosing what they wear, what they play with, how fun time should be spent) so that they don't need to exercise their independence at the dinner table.

Copycat fads.

These are common in younger siblings who copy their older brothers and sisters. The best solution is to ignore them – they soon pass, particularly if they get no response.

Anxiety fads.

Your child might refuse to eat pork after seeing the film *Babe*, or chicken after *Chicken Little*. These types of anxiety fade over time, so just leave the food in the short term.

Strange foods.

Children can be very conservative about trying something new. Give them time, and continue to persist. Introduce different foods a little at a time, so that they are not hit with a completely new menu all in one go.

Allergy or intolerance fads.

A child might know instinctively that a certain food will make him physically ill. If a child repeatedly and violently rejects a food, it is worth having him checked for food allergies.

What can you do?

- Don't make a fuss at mealtimes. There will be times when a child is starving and will demolish anything in sight. At other times, he will pick and graze and seem to need nothing substantial. Go with the flow. Never force a child to clear his plate. He'll grow up associating food with stress and bad behaviour.
- If your child genuinely doesn't like something – mushrooms, for example – don't force it. Suggest that he tries one bite. If you're trying something new and he claims not to be very hungry, suggest three bites of everything on the plate. Children need to learn to try foods, and they need to eat a variety of good foods in order to stay healthy.
- Show some respect. We all have foods we don't like, and there are very healthy eaters who simply cannot abide a particular vegetable, meat or flavour. Don't force food that a child dislikes. The problem with faddy eaters, of course, is that they claim not to like anything. That's a different scenario. If your child eats well, tries new things and eats a healthy, varied diet, then the odd 'no-way' food can be dropped from the daily diet. But don't give up. Try new recipes. Introduce it again in a month's time. Children's tastes change and what may have been considered revolting one week may be the new favourite later on. If your child rejects a food after trying it a number of times, and continues to dislike it, leave it for a period of time.
- Don't offer alternatives. Serve a healthy meal for the whole family and don't panic if your child doesn't eat much. If he is hungry, he will eat. Even the most resolute child will not starve himself to death.
- Invite a good eater round for dinner – often! Children like to do what their peers are doing, and if that involves eating new foods, they'll do it.
- Educate children. Explain what foods are healthy and what they do for our bodies. Fruits and vegetables make colds go away, make us concentrate better, make us faster runners, for example. Don't be boring, but put these facts in terms a child will understand.
- Don't label children. Parents and carers often create self-fulfilling prophecies. If a child is accused of being picky, he will be. If you continually praise a child during meals for what he does eat, and insist to everyone around that your child is such a good eater, he'll take some pride in this achievement.
- Don't give up. Picky eaters are often picky because we allow them to be. If you give in and serve only what a child will eat, you will be setting up unhealthy eating patterns that can run through life. Serve healthy meals at every sitting. Offer the normal treats, and balance the good with the bad parts of his diet.

- Empower children. If a child feels that he's lost control, he'll dig in his heels or revert to tears or tantrums. Make up a list of eight or nine healthy meals, with a variety of different vegetables on the side. Let each child in the family choose a particular night's menu. You can suggest that there have to be at least four fruits or vegetables with every meal, and at least two have to be different from the meal chosen for the previous night. If you make it into a game, children will be more likely to become involved. They'll also feel that they have some control.
- Introduce new foods alongside the old favourites, and then slowly drop the parts of a child's diet that concern you most. Don't be tempted to launch a dramatically different eating programme overnight. You'll incite mutiny. Instead, make small changes. Every new food that your child eats is a step in the right direction.
- Introduce a star chart for younger children. They can be encouraged to put a star up for every healthy or new food they eat. When they reach an agreed total, you can offer a treat.
- If you have a grazer on your hands, make sure that the snacks he eats are nutritious. Some children just cannot seem to stomach a big meal and prefer to eat little and often throughout the day. This style of eating is fine, as long as the foods eaten are nutritious and balanced. But whatever your child eats throughout the day, sit him down and make sure he eats it at the table. You don't want to encourage eating on the run, which can develop into a bad habit. If he's had plenty of small meals throughout the day, he won't want a big dinner, but serve smaller portions of whatever you are serving the rest of the family.
- If a child refuses food or just picks at his food for a long time, don't push it. Don't make a child feel guilty if he's just not hungry, and don't ever make him eat to please you. This sort of emotional blackmail can lower a child's self-esteem and make him insecure.
- Eat the same foods as the children in your care. There should be no distinction between children's food and adult food. Good, healthy food is appropriate for the whole family. If children see their parents enjoying a broad range of foods, they'll be more likely to try some.
- Picky parents are more likely to produce picky children. Try to expand your own diet to include foods that you don't normally eat. You might find that your tastes have changed, too. Don't only serve foods that you like. Try new recipes and be more adventurous. What you want to aim for is variety.
- Faddy eating is just that – a fad. However, it can grow into something more problematic if it is not addressed early on. Almost all young children will exercise their will by choosing not to eat certain foods, and they will also reject new things as a matter of course. The key is to remain patient but firm, to avoid making mealtimes a battleground by creating issues around food, and to persevere.
- No child will willingly starve himself, and all will develop a liking for new foods as they get older. If you pander to a fad, you'll create a child who develops negative associations with food, and who remains unwilling to try anything different from the usual fare – an unhealthy scenario no matter how you look at it.

Chapter 11: Faddy Eaters

The power of peer pressure

According to Professor Fergus Lowe, a psychologist at the University of Wales in Bangor, who for the past nine years has been exploring ways to get children to eat more healthily, 'peer pressure is very powerful'.

Professor Lowe has discovered that fussy eaters can be transformed into fruit and veg champions if they are just given a little encouragement. He shows them a short 'Food Dude' video starring animated characters and child actors. The 'Food Dudes' are fruit- and veg-munching heroes who fight the baddie 'Junk Food Junta' and make the world a better place. Next, Professor Lowe gives the children little rewards, such as Food Dude stickers and hats, for eating up their greens. 'It works extremely well,' he says. 'The reason why children don't eat fruit and vegetables is, to a large extent, down to peer pressure and advertising, which creates a culture that's very negative about fruit and veg. We aim to change the culture, so that it becomes a trendy thing to do, then you get all that peer pressure on your side'.

In one of the professor's home-based studies with fussy eaters (aged between five and six), children's consumption of targeted fruit rose from 4% to 100%, and targeted vegetables from 1% to 8%. Targeted fruit consumption was still at 100% and vegetable consumption at 5% when the children were observed again six months later. In day-care nursery settings results were equally impressive, as they were in primary schools.

Key points

- Most children will develop food fads at some point, as part of the developmental process and becoming independent.
- Peer pressure has an enormous impact, and most children will want to eat what their friends are eating, which can make the job difficult for parents and carers.
- Educating children through fun means can help them to see the benefits of healthy foods.
- Remaining calm and refusing to allow food to become an issue is the best solution.
- Continue to offer only the foods you want your child to eat, and no alternatives. No child will starve himself, and his tastes will change as he becomes older.

Chapter 12

Go to sleep!

More parents complain about their children's sleeping habits than any other issue. Night-time waking, inability to get to sleep, regular trips from the bed and even nightmares are the source of great parental frustration and debate. They are also the source of broken sleep, which seems to affect parents far more than it does the children themselves. But affect children they do! Sleep problems impact on mood, concentration, behaviour and overall health. The good news is that there are plenty of tricks to get children to sleep – and keep them there.

Why is sleep important?

It's actually more important than you might think. All of us need good, restful sleep, but for children it's absolutely essential. Inadequate sleep lowers the immune response. A recent study showed that missing even a few hours a night on a regular basis can decrease the number of natural killer cells, which are responsible for fighting off invaders such as bacteria and viruses.

Even occasional sleeping problems can make daily life feel more stressful or cause a child to be less productive. A survey in the US showed that children who get enough sleep are better able to concentrate, accomplish required tasks and handle minor irritations. In contrast, those regularly getting less sleep than required showed impairment of the ability to perform tasks involving memory, learning, logical reasoning and mathematical calculation. They also found relationships at home and with friends more difficult.

Growth hormones are released during sleep, and while it is unknown what effect this has on growth patterns in children, research has shown that children who are chronically sleep-deprived have retarded growth. There is also evidence that abused children do not grow well because they wake too often to get sufficient sleep. When the same children sleep well in a more secure environment, their growth and development improve.

How much sleep does a child need?

Sleep needs differ dramatically between children, just as they do between adults. However, sleep is crucially important in childhood, and there are very few children who do not need to get at least the average required hours. Two-year-olds, for example, need fourteen hours of sleep – broken across naps and night-time sleep. Three- to six- year-olds need ten to twelve hours across a 24-hour period. Given that the nap usually makes its departure around the age of three, a good, long night-time sleep is crucial.

Establishing routines

The key to successful sleep habits for children of all ages is a sound pre-sleep routine undertaken on a daily basis. Children feel secure when they know their boundaries and what to expect. If the rules and routines shift repeatedly they'll feel unsettled and will be more likely to create a fuss or waken in the night. A bedtime routine needs to be calm. It can be difficult for parents who have been away from their children all day to avoid boisterous playtime, but the sheer excitement of having a parent return home, coupled with some rough and tumble, tickling or chasing, can make it impossible to settle your child down to sleep.

If you do return home later, keep things low-key. Settle down with a story and a drink, or even just a little chat. Play some soft music and take time to relax yourself. As your child gets older, they will welcome this peaceful period and you'll build up a good rapport if they know this time is always allotted to them. This can be quiet time – a time for praise, gentle activities and comfort. If you are stressed or tired after work, try not to let it show. Never use this time to air disagreements or inflict discipline. It's certainly acceptable to talk things through – perhaps your toddler had a bad day at nursery – but keep things calm. If you are too enthusiastic, excited or angry, they will react in kind. No child will sleep well if he is anxious or over-excited.

Creating the optimum sleep environment

A child's bedroom is an important part of restful sleep. Children need to feel comfortable and relaxed in order to sleep through the night. Like adults, they need to sleep in an environment that is free of distractions. It's not surprising that children resist going to sleep and wake at ungodly hours to play when their room is full of tantalising toys or favourite playthings. The answer is to keep the bedroom as clutter-free as possible.

Many children like to fill their beds with books and toys, but it's not a good idea to encourage this. By all means suggest a comforting book at bedtime, but if it's something interactive or likely to keep them awake, keep it away from the bed. Many children have a blanket or a soft toy that they associate with sleep, which experts believe is a useful tool for encouraging sleep, particularly in young children. If you can keep a familiar item in the bed, they'll learn to associate it with comfort and with sleep.

Naps

Paradoxically, regular naps will help to encourage good night-time sleep habits by making falling asleep a routine part of life. Young children do need a great deal of sleep and it is unlikely they will get enough in the night-time hours alone. To help your child fall asleep at a reasonable hour, don't let him nap past 3-4 pm. At least four hours should elapse between the end of an afternoon nap and bedtime. If you make nap times a part of a daily routine, in the same way that you set bedtimes, your child will learn to know what to expect and will feel comforted by the regular routine.

Bedtimes

Many toddlers do not seem tired late at night and get a second wind, appearing hyperactive and full of energy. This is a clear indication that your child is over-tired and needs to be settled. Most parents find that settling children before the 8.30 pm witching hour can make a big difference. In fact, if you have a baby or toddler who finds it difficult to get to sleep, try bringing bedtime forward by a half an hour. It sounds simple, but it works in the large majority of cases.

Signs of sleepiness

It can be difficult to assess when a child is ready for bed, and it's important to learn to recognise signs of sleepiness. In young babies, pulling ears, crying, rubbing eyes or even developing dark circles around the eyes are an indication of a need for sleep. Try to act quickly when you see these signs. If you wait it out, they'll be much less likely to settle. Older children may become tearful, over-energetic and demanding when they need some rest. They may not seem remotely tired, but a burst of energy signals that sleep is required and you should head into the bedtime routine as quickly as possible.

Troubleshooting

Put a fairly rigid routine into place, and stick with it. As boring as it may seem, try to keep things even and organised, with activities and meals taking place at the same times every day - at least until things settle down.

- Don't let children fall asleep in the car! Hum, sing, nudge, chat – anything you have to do to keep him awake. If a child still naps, make sure the regular routine is followed. Be prepared for some irritability
- Settle them down early to bed. An appropriate bedtime for most children is 7.30 pm. In fact, one study showed that 8.00 pm is the latest that any child under the age of fourteen should be heading off to sleep. If they don't fall asleep naturally, read a story or give them a book to look at. Put on a story tape or some gentle music. Make sure they know you mean business. If you allow them to climb out of bed and join in the activities in other parts of the house, you'll never instil good sleeping habits.
- You might need to sit in the bedroom to ensure they stay put. Don't be tempted to engage in conversation. Many children become more relaxed in the evenings and ready to talk about problems, concerns, or even their school day. You want to encourage this type of communication, which is why it's important to introduce a period of quiet chatting into a good bedtime routine. However, some children learn that they can get and keep your attention by bringing up concerns and will do everything they can to engage you in conversation simply to stay up later. Beware of this ploy.
- Obviously, if your child suddenly wants to talk about something serious that has not been previously divulged, you'll have to bend your rules. But stay calm, open and positive and let them know that you take their concerns seriously.
- Introduce a star chart or another reward system for children who stay in their beds. Offer plenty of praise when they go to sleep at a reasonable time.
- Wake them up in the morning at the normal time. They may be tired, groggy or irritable, but it will help to establish the right kinds of patterns.

Chapter 12: Go to sleep!

Refusing to go to bed

Most children clue into the fact that the fun doesn't stop when they go to bed, and they may be reluctant to miss out on anything, particularly if they have older siblings who are permitted to stay up later. Offer choices so that your child feels in control: choosing pyjamas, a cup for water, a story and even bedtime (within an agreed period of time).

- Show them the clock and put them in charge of remembering when it's time to go up to bed. Given a little responsibility, children normally rise to the occasion and are scrupulously honest.
- Make sure there isn't any real reason why they don't want to go to bed. Are they having nightmares? Try to spend some time talking to your child each night to allay any fears. Promise to come back into the room in five minutes to check on them, making sure that you do.
- Practise some advance planning to counter any delaying tactics - another story, another glass of water, a trip to the loo, another kiss goodnight, a hug. If they are toilet training, you'll have to agree to loo trips, but make it clear that you are not falling for a planned escape.
- Make his bedroom a sanctuary, with cosy blankets and a familiar cuddly toy. Tuck him in and make sure that he is comfortable and content. Stay with him for a few minutes so that he doesn't feel that he is being sent away.
- Wind down well before you want him to go to bed. Make sure that the television is off and that all fun has ceased at least 20 minutes before bedtime.
- Make it clear the rest of the family are not up to wildly fun activities while he goes to bed. If he knows there isn't anything exciting at hand he will feel happier about being on his own.
- Above all, be firm and consistent. If you give in once, you'll be setting the stage for recurrent battles. While it's never a good idea to show anger at bedtime, which may cause your child to have a troubled sleep, you can make it clear, without losing your temper, that you don't find his actions remotely amusing.
- Praise, praise, praise. When he goes to bed when you ask, make a big fuss and show him how happy and proud you are. When he argues or refuses to go to bed, ignore the behaviour that you don't want to encourage.

Can't fall asleep?

If your child will go to bed, but can't get to sleep, you'll have to adopt a different approach:

- Is your child genuinely tired? He may not be physically tired enough to get to sleep. Make sure he is getting enough exercise in the day and that nap times are not pushing bedtime further on.
- He may be overtired. Extreme activity in the evenings is a good sign he will find it difficult to get to sleep. Move bedtime forward by a half an hour, and make sure the bedtime routine is soothing.
- If they are under stress for any reason (school, difficulties with friends, parental divorce or unhappiness, for example), children may not be relaxed enough to get to sleep. Try to

take time to talk things through as part of a routine, and keep it calm and positive. Work out strategies to make things easier and let your child know that you are on his side.

Night waking

Some children and even adults find it difficult to go back to sleep if they have woken during the night and will need encouragement to do so. Childhood is a period of enormous development, so don't be surprised if your child suddenly starts waking at night. He may be over-stimulated by the excitement of the day, and find it difficult to settle and to stay asleep. At these times, it's all the more important to implement a good winding-down routine.

Providing a comfort object, such as a favourite blanket or cuddly toy can help. Many children just want the reassurance of the familiar when they waken in the dark. Some children seem determined to cry unless they have a particular parent to settle them. From the earliest days, ensure that both parents or even other family members play a role in settling a child back to sleep.

Key points

- Lack of sleep can affect all aspects of a child's health and development.
- Many children are not getting enough sleep - largely because parents are unaware of how much they need and give in to demands too easily.
- A strong routine is the most important element of good sleep habits.
- Do not give in to a child's demands - stick to your guns and be loving but firm at bedtime.

Chapter 13

Hitting

Young children often lash out and hit out of frustration or anger, through learned behaviour, or simply as a means of expressing themselves. They may, in fact, be playing rather than anything more sinister. While this type of aggression is disturbing, it is not unexpected, and there are many ways parents and carers can put a stop to hitting. These include understanding why children exhibit the behaviour, teaching children more appropriate ways to communicate, and using a consistent team approach to combat it.

When a child hits, it is often difficult to understand the motivation. The younger the child, the more likely it is that he is simply playing, mimicking behaviour he has seen at home or on television, or acting out a negative emotion, such as anger, frustration, sadness, insecurity or fear. Older children hit for different reasons, and they may lack the social skills or self-control to manage their behaviour. In both scenarios, however, children need to be taught that hitting is not appropriate behaviour, and given the tools with which to express themselves in non-violent ways.

Age differences

Toddlers are too young to understand the idea of sharing, and naturally believe that everything they touch belongs to them, and that everything they want should be instantly theirs. The frustration they feel, and the outrage at not getting their own way is often manifested in hitting episodes. Most aggressive acts occur over toys or as a result of not getting what they want.

Children aged between two and five years old are self-centred and have not developed all the brain connections needed to see another person's point of view. They also tend to see things as all or nothing, meaning they do not understand that someone is not all good, or not all bad. Young children also have difficulty thinking about the future or planning for it – instant gratification is the main motivation for most of them and waiting is not normally a consideration. Young children also have difficulties sorting out fantasy from reality and will become genuinely confused about what is real on television. Even cartoons for youngsters can be full of violence and hitting – and when those actions raise a laugh or encourage applause, they will be in no doubt that these are actions to be repeated.

Most importantly, however, children all have different temperaments. Some are easily inflamed, lively and quick to react, while others are gentle and accepting. Children with more difficult or feisty temperaments have difficulty reading the small cues that other children send out in social situations. For example, a more aggressive child may consider a child coming to join his game of trains as a usurper or intruder and not see that there are no hostile intentions whatsoever.

Chapter 13: Hitting

All young children lack the ability to empathise and will never truly understand how you or anyone else feels until they develop this skill and emotion. If you are angry with children, they may cry and be frightened. However, this is more likely to be because you raised your voice or looked angry, rather than the fact that they empathised with you or understood how you were feeling. And remember, too, that little children do not know how to feel sorry. While it is important to teach a child to say sorry, and to apologise once he is able to string together two to three words (this reinforces the lesson that he should not act without considering the effect of his behaviour on others, and teaches the basics of empathy), he will not truly understand the concept of empathy or feel genuinely sorry until between 3 and 5 years of age.

A culture of violence

Considering the violent and aggressive behaviours that children witness while watching television, or the intimate exposure to violent family rows, or acts of violence (muggings, burglaries, bullying and even murder) committed openly in our communities, we should not be surprised to see children behave in aggressive ways.

It is important, therefore, to teach kindness, empathy and compassion, to avoid young children witnessing physical violence in the home or on television and games consoles, and to model the behaviour you want a child to exhibit. Children who are persistently aggressive and cannot seem to get the message that hitting is not acceptable may be demonstrating behaviours that may be the result of one or many factors:

- early insecure or disorganized attachment.
- victimisation.
- witnessing violence.
- receiving rewards or approval for aggressive behaviour.

These are issues that may require specialist attention.

What to do

- It is extremely important to teach children that anger is not bad but that expressing it by hitting is not acceptable. Young children are likely to take it out on others when they become angry. It is this behaviour that needs to be changed, not the emotion.
- Some children grow up ashamed of their feelings because they have been taught that it is bad to feel or show anger. It is emotionally healthier for children to learn that everyone has angry feelings at times and that there are appropriate ways to express anger.
- Remind yourself that a child who hits is not bad, but his behaviour is. So it is important to draw attention to the negative behaviour and to let a child know that his actions are not acceptable. He must, however, still feel valued and liked, but do not go overboard.
- Children who get attention through hitting will continue the behaviour – particularly if they are not getting enough attention elsewhere. Instead, make a big show of praising good and expected behaviour, so that they learn what is right and what is wrong.

- It can be helpful to look at books about anger and hitting, such as *I Feel Angry* by Brian Moses and Mike Gordon, published by Hodder Wayland, or *Poemotions: Poems About Being Angry - I Want to Shout and Stamp About* by Tony Mitton and Mike Gordon published by Hodder Children's Books. Use them as starting points to discuss ways to get rid of anger without hurting other people. At the older end of the age scale, children are bound to have plenty of ideas.
- Very young children often need help putting words to what they are feeling. Hitting and lashing-out can often be the result of frustration. Help them to express emotion, giving them words, such as sad, angry, frustrated, cross, lonely, jealous. If they can discuss their feelings, they are much less likely to resort to violence.
- Good role models for children are always the best teachers. If you lash out, even on the odd occasion, children are likely to follow suit. You will teach children to use violent behaviour to express angry feelings. Instead, take the time to explain when you are angry and how you are feeling. If children hear you using words to express your anger, they are likely to do the same.
- Encourage children to learn to get rid of angry feelings through vigorous physical activity such as running, digging, punching a pillow, or tearing an old newspaper.
- Distract! Young children will forget about angry feelings or frustration quickly, particularly if something seems more exciting.
- Make sure that you and your carers or partners are consistent. My own 12-month-old baby started to hit whenever he was angry or frustrated, despite my clear displeasure. I later learned that my older sons made a game of it with him and laughed when he hit. Lack of consistency was the problem here – two different responses are confusing for any child.
- Diffuse a situation by suggesting soothing activities, such as a bath, playing in a paddling pool or a sink of warm water, playing with play dough, finger painting or playing in the sand.
- Although it is difficult to be physically affectionate with young children in your care these days, it is worth using closeness to calm a child and to make them feel good about themselves. A child who is out of control may just need some reassurance that they are loved. Soothing and comforting can go a long way.
- Sometimes the fit between a particular child and their child-care setting is poor. If you think that a setting is wrong for your child or a child in your care, for example if you think it is too regimented, too busy and noisy, or not warm and personal enough, then a change is probably warranted.
- Aggressive behaviours are learned. Responsive caregivers establish an atmosphere of cooperation and caring.
- Remember that a child who regularly hits may be witness to inappropriate behaviour at home, and it can be difficult to balance this. In this situation, all you can do is to ensure that he understands the rules of your home/classroom/nursery, and realise that this behaviour is inappropriate.
- Dealing calmly with children when they misbehave is important. But sometimes we still feel anger. Children are accurate observers of body language so they are aware of our

own anger and frustration. Reassure the children that you are angry at the situation or behaviour and not at them.

- When a child hurts someone, focus most of your attention on the child who was hurt. Comfort the child. Avoid rewarding the child who was hitting with your attention.
- If possible, have the child who was aggressive help the other child. Instead of a forced hug and a meaningless: 'I'm sorry', you might ask the aggressor to give the victim a soft animal to hug. Compassion and regret need to be learned, but you can help by making clear that even young children need to take responsibility for their actions.
- Examine your home, nursery or centre for potential sources of frustration and accidental anger. How crowded are the indoor and outdoor play spaces? Are there enough materials? Are the materials age-appropriate? Do the children have enough time to get really involved in the play? Are there enough adults available to provide positive attention to the children? Are children expected to sit quietly for longer periods of time than their attention span allows?
- Watch out for inappropriate television shows or games. The less violence a child witnesses, the less chance there is that he will act it out or believe that it is acceptable.

Remember that many children lash out when they feel powerless. They cannot get what they want and they see no other way to express how they are feeling. Empower children as much as you can, offer little jobs suitable to their age, give regular responsibilities and set expectations that are achievable. If a child feels good about himself, he will be much less likely to hit. Empower children by teaching them the best ways to express feelings. A child who can get his message across without resorting to violence will be happier in any situation.

Key points

- A child who hits is not necessarily a violent or problem child. Young children hit out of frustration, anger and impatience.
- Many children use hitting to express themselves before they know how to do so verbally. We can help by teaching them words and appropriate actions.
- Young children do not understand empathy or even the word 'sorry' until later in their development. In this case it is important to simply teach that hitting is wrong. End of story.
- Always model the behaviours you want to see – a child who sees an adult lash out will do so, particularly if he is rewarded by attention.

Chapter 14

Hyperactivity

Toddlers and pre-schoolers are, by nature, brimming with energy and enthusiasm, and even the most patient parent and carer can be run ragged by constant questions, demands and lively outbursts. It is becoming increasingly common to label over-energetic children as hyperactive or ADHD, but before you pack a pre-schooler off for the widely prescribed drug Ritalin, let's look at what is normal, and what you can do to calm a child whose energy levels would support the national grid.

ADHD?

Most parents and carers are aware of differences in ADHD (attention deficit and hyperactivity disorder) children from an early age. Hyperactivity is only one ray of the spectrum, but it is often the basis on which diagnosis is (usually incorrectly) made. ADHD children often lose interest and dart off even during a favourite activity or television programme – they may even disappear during a game, apparently forgetting that they were even involved.

Some sufferers tear around, out of control, and display manic behaviour which appears to be impossible to restrain, but others may be docile and quiet, even co-operative, with other classic symptoms. At present, ADHD is a diagnosis applied to children who consistently display certain characteristic behaviours over a period of time. The most common behaviours fall into three categories: inattention, hyperactivity and impulsivity.

Inattention

Most children can be inattentive from time to time, and the attention span of the average pre-schooler may only be four or five minutes (although this increases, year by year, as they get older). ADHD children, however, may become bored with a task after only a few minutes. They may give effortless, automatic attention to activities and things they enjoy. But focusing deliberate, conscious attention to organising and completing a task or learning something new is difficult.

Hyperactivity

Children who are hyperactive always seem to be in motion. They cannot sit still. Hyperactive children squirm in their seat or roam around the room. Or they might wiggle their feet, touch everything or noisily tap their toys, crayons or even fingers.

Impulsivity

Children who are overly impulsive seem unable to curb their immediate reactions or think before they act. They may blurt out inappropriate comments, or they may run out into the street without looking. Their impulsivity may make it hard for them to wait for things they want or to take their turn in games. They may grab a toy from another child or hit when they are upset.

Chapter 14: Hyperactivity

Not every child who is overly hyperactive, inattentive or impulsive has an attention disorder. Since most children sometimes blurt out things they did not mean to say, bounce from one task to another, or become disorganised and forgetful, how can specialists tell if the problem is ADHD?

To assess whether a child has ADHD, specialists consider several critical questions. Are these behaviours excessive, long-term and pervasive? That is, do they occur more often than in other people the same age? Are they a continuous problem, not just a response to a temporary situation? Do the behaviours occur in several settings or only in one specific place, such as the playground?

Could it be something else?

The fact is that many things can produce these behaviours in children. Anything from chronic fear to mild seizures can make a child seem overactive, quarrelsome, impulsive or inattentive. For example, a formerly co-operative child who becomes overactive and easily distracted after a parent's death is dealing with an emotional problem, not ADHD. A chronic middle ear infection can also make a child seem distracted. So can living with family members who are physically abusive or addicted to drugs or alcohol. A child who is completely unable to concentrate or hold attention may well have something serious worrying him.

In other children, ADHD-like behaviours may be their response to a defeating situation. Perhaps the child has a learning disability and is not developmentally ready to learn to read and write at the time these are taught in a pre-school classroom. Or maybe the work is too hard or too easy, leaving the child frustrated or bored. Many young children are being taught literacy and numeracy in classroom-like situations, and many of those children are simply not ready.

It is also important to realise that, during certain stages of development, the majority of children that age tend to be inattentive, hyperactive, or impulsive – but do not have ADHD. Pre-schoolers have lots of energy and run everywhere they go, but this does not mean they are hyperactive. And even the majority of teenagers go through a phase when they are messy, disorganised, and reject authority. It does not mean they will have a lifelong problem controlling their impulses.

Finally, consider that hearing impairment can cause many of the symptoms of both ADHD and high energy, as can depression or anxiety. It is important to watch out for changes in behaviour before you label a child.

Normal energy

It is important to remember that in adult life, energy is considered an asset – a much envied quality that many successful people manage to channel into rewarding careers and active lifestyles. Many hyperactive children will grow into energetic adults, so it is important that this natural energy or spirit is not quashed in an attempt to make a child conform. Some children are simply lucky recipients of a dynamic energy that will one day enable them to be successful.

ADHD children, however, have other qualities that make education, friendships, interaction, learning and developing difficult, and for this reason you should report your suspicions to parents. A GP is usually the first port of call, and a referral to a specialist will normally follow. No carer, parent, teacher or even GP is fully equipped to make an accurate diagnosis.

Dealing with excessive energy

It is beyond the scope of this book to discuss ways of dealing with ADHD children, but even diagnosed hyperactive children will respond to the following tips:

Sleep

Unlike adults, many over-tired children do not fall asleep in a corner – they break into a second, third and fourth wind, and carry on running. If a child in your care is consistently over-active in between yawns, talk to his parents about his sleeping patterns. Even an extra hour or so can make a big difference to behaviour. Interestingly, many over-tired children find it difficult to get to sleep at night. Moving bedtime just thirty minutes earlier can help them to settle before they are 'past it'.

Diet

There is no question that food additives, caffeine and sugar affect children's behaviour, and the classic birthday party 'high' is evidence enough. If your hyperactive charge comes in at full throttle, has a tearful, sleepy trough, and then perks up again after chocolate biscuits, he is likely to be sensitive to some elements of his diet. Encourage parents to provide wholesome breakfasts, with as little sugar as possible, and offer plain oat biscuits and water at break time.

Attention span

All children's attention spans are different, and they will also vary according to a child's upbringing. If he has never had to sit down and concentrate on any one thing for a period of time, he will be unused to doing so, and will be likely to have a much shorter attention span than his peers. To help lengthen the time a child can stay engaged in an activity, begin where he is now and take small steps towards a long-term goal. If your child can stay on task for two minutes now, work on increasing that time to three or four minutes before you expect him to be able to focus for five. What sit-down activities does the child enjoy? That is where you will begin.

If he likes puzzles, take time to do puzzles every day. If he likes you to read out loud, try to read more often. If he enjoys imaginary play, try to find time to get down on the floor and play with dolls or action figures. Whatever the activity, try to spend fifteen minutes every day with the child without interruptions. You will probably notice that he is better able to continue playing if he knows that you will not get up and leave just because he is not asking for interaction. This may be difficult in a nursery or group setting, but it can be undertaken in small groups, or occasionally with a helper.

Demonstrate

Show children how to do things. Do not just explain things and expect them to understand. Children with high energy may have very short attention spans, and may not take on board what you are telling them. They may need something practical and visual, such as a demonstration, in order to get the message. For example, telling a hyperactive child to put away the toys may end up with more mess than you had bargained for. Sit down and show him how and where to put things away, and gently discourage play in the process. It helps to teach the difference between playtime and tidy time.

Let children move around

Give children opportunities to move around. Children need to be able to channel their energy, or it will burst out at inappropriate moments. Ensure that no activity lasts longer than about fifteen minutes without a break of some sort. Even a rudimentary exercise session, with some toe-touching and stretching, can help to relieve the build-up of energy. A good run in the playground, park or garden should be a part of every daily routine.

Simple routine

Make your daily routine as simple and straightforward as possible. It will help to keep the child calmer and he will have more chance of remembering what comes next. Try to avoid rushing around or eating on the hop, which will make him feel unsettled.

Distinguish between hyperactivity and bad behaviour

Remember that hyperactivity is not bad behaviour. There can be learning difficulties present, and some children may have some difficulty with co-ordination or controlling movement.

One-to-one attention

Some studies show that children with a tendency towards hyperactivity benefit from increased attention on a one-to-one basis. Many children are labelled difficult, hyperactive or hard work when they first exhibit these symptoms, and in some cases this can create a self-fulfilling prophecy. This type of negative labelling can harm a child emotionally, so it is important to offer positive reinforcement and to raise a child's self-esteem. There should be a period of quality time in which positive behaviour can be reinforced.

Appropriate discipline

Discipline should never be harsh, as an overactive child is not usually wilfully being naughty, but simply losing control. Removing a child from the scene of a tantrum or an outburst, or whatever behaviour has got out of control, will help. Time out seems to help with some hyperactive children.

Exercise

Some children naturally have increased energy and physical requirements, and it is important for any child with these tendencies to get plenty of exercise. This can mean a break not offered to other children in a school environment. If a child is extremely active, it may well be that early schooling is not appropriate. Many children are not able to handle the confines of school environment until they are older, and it can exacerbate a problem if they start too early. If you feel that a child in your charge is not dealing well with a group situation or is being pushed to attend school too early, it is worth discussing the alternatives with parents.

Although it can be enormously frustrating to keep tabs on an overly energetic child, it is important that you do not immediately assume that he is hyperactive or suffering from attention deficit disorder. Most children have periods where their concentration slips, and where energy overcomes logic, courtesy and self-control. If the problem is long-standing, however, it is worth mentioning your concerns to a child's parents.

But remember, all children require an outlet – periods in their routine, every day, where they are allowed to express themselves, let off steam and simply be children. Discipline is important, but no child is psychologically or physically wired to sit still and be good for extended periods of time. If you stick to a firm routine – with plenty of enthusiasm, expression and time off for exercise – while gently working on extending attention span, most children will respond with appropriate behaviour at appropriate times.

Key points

- ADHD is a diagnosable condition with several key factors, including hyperactivity, impulsiveness and inattention; however, it must be diagnosed by a trained professional and any concerns should be relayed to parents.
- All children exhibit the classic signs of ADHD at some point during normal development, and it is important not to assume that all over-energy is indicative of a problem.
- Develop a strong routine, with plenty of time for children to express themselves and to run off their energy.
- Examine your expectations – children must be allowed to be wild from time to time and to be children. If they are expected to sit still for long periods of time, most will fidget, lose interest and even lash out.
- Work on improving and extending attention span with plenty of interactive, one-to-one, or small group activities. Children respond better when they are given encouragement, and they soon understand what is expected of them.

Chapter 15

I can't ...

Most young children show some independence and actively engage with their peers and with toys and other equipment. They enjoy the process of learning about and then mastering a task, and will repeat it over and over again. Many are intrepid, and believe that they can accomplish anything, no matter how difficult it may seem at the outset. But some children are certain they cannot do things for themselves, and constantly demand assistance with even the smallest and most achievable tasks. 'I can't do it,' is a common complaint.

After an illness, or a negative or traumatic experience, many children will exhibit helplessness and require more assistance than usual for a short time. However, when this behaviour continues over time, children may have learned to be helpless and dependent, and this is a quality that can spill over into older childhood and even adulthood. The psychological term for this type of behaviour is 'learned helplessness', and children can experience different degrees, depending upon their background and the encouragement they get.

Learned helplessness was identified by Martin Seligman, who found that a state of apathy may develop if children perceive little or no connection between their actions and their outcomes. Another good study that shows this effect was undertaken with eight-week-old infants. When they moved their heads on pressure-sensitive pillows, a brightly coloured mobile overhead rotated. The infants clearly enjoyed this activity, for they smiled and cooed whenever they caused the mobile to turn. A second group of infants was exposed to the same situation – with one important difference; they had no control over their mobiles, which rotated periodically on their own.

Infants in the second group were at first fascinated by the rotating mobile, but soon became a bit bored and apathetic. They rarely smiled at the object and were not particularly interested in watching it turn. Later the researchers exposed all the babies to mobiles that they could control by moving their heads. Children who had previously learned to control mobiles were soon turning their heads and exercising control again.

However, the babies who had not been able to control the mobiles in the earlier session made no further attempts to exercise control, even though they now had the opportunity to do so. Apparently these children learned that they were powerless to influence their environment, so they gave up and accepted their learned helplessness.

Learning about the controllability of events is an important aspect of human development. When children get no response from their environment, or fail to master things on their own, they lose interest and self-belief. They simply stop trying and often become unresponsive. Some studies show that babies of depressed mothers are more likely to suffer from learned helplessness later in life; other children are given little opportunity to try things for themselves and therefore lose the belief that they can succeed.

Most young children are hugely optimistic, and believe they can succeed at any task just because they want to – this theory has been documented in several studies. But learned helplessness has been observed in children as young as four, and even in babies, as we have seen above.

What is the key?

The way in which adults react to children's successes and failures has been found to influence the way a child views his own competence. In other words, the way that children interpret success and failure determines their behaviour. So when a child has learned to be helpless, for whatever reason, adults need to react to him in a way that encourages him to believe in himself and to learn new behaviour.

Who is to blame?

Learned helplessness is a motivational problem. It may be caused when a child has failed in a task or two in the past, causing him to believe that he is incapable of doing anything.

Studies show that if children feel as though they cannot control their environment, this feeling will impair learning in various situations. There is plenty of research showing that learned helplessness is caused by parents and or teachers who may (even unwittingly) have indicated that a child's failures are caused by lack of competence rather than suggesting that he is not trying hard enough.

Is it serious?

Learned helplessness can be very serious – for a number of reasons. Children develop a lack of self-confidence in challenging tasks that results in deterioration of performance. They also use poor problem-solving strategies; their attention wanders and they feel that they are struggling for nothing.

In some cases, this helplessness is perceived to be a lack of ability, and children are held back a year, which can affect social skills. In the end, they get a message that they are worthless and hopeless – they feel incompetent and unable to master any new material or task. Learned helpless children 'know' that they are failures and will not think otherwise. Moreover, children with few successes will feel inferior, which leads to low self-esteem. Later on, most give up trying to gain respect through their academic performance so they turn to other means for recognition. They may become the class clown, bully or tease. In adolescence, they try to gain respect through antisocial behaviours.

What should you do?

- One researcher found that when a child succeeds at any task, adults should praise his ability. He claimed that success must be attributed to ability rather than luck or even hard work. This is necessary for children to believe that they are capable, and that it was their own capability that led to success.

- Hard work is also important, of course. If children find it difficult to succeed at a task, you need to emphasise the fact that the child is capable and just needs to try a little harder. One of the main characteristics of helpless children is that they give up at the slightest provocation. Nudging towards completion is important – but equally important is instilling a belief that a child can do it.
- By placing the focus on insufficient effort, children eventually learn that they can change the outcome. Children can control effort, and feel empowered and enabled to try when they are in control.
- Do not assume that providing a child with a host of successful experiences will work. Many studies have shown that experiencing repeated success is not enough to change behaviour.
- Children need to be trained to attribute success to ability – and failure to lack of effort. In other words, they need to believe that when they are successful, it is because they are good enough and able enough – but that lack of success does not mean they are not able, just that they have not tried hard enough.
- So teachers and parents need to address success with compliments about ability and unsuccessful attempts with comments about effort. Good examples include: 'You use scissors very well – what a good cutter!' or, 'You know a lot about dinosaurs.' If a child is not successful, you might say: 'Try a little harder, you almost did it,' or, 'It takes practice to finish this job but you can do it if you try your hardest'.
- It is important to understand that learned helplessness is absolutely no indication of talent or being bright. It is simply a behaviour that has been learned over time. All of us want to produce children who have self-belief and will go out there and try – and the key to that is teaching them to persist and persist with tasks until they learn that they do have control over the outcome.
- The way you speak to children can also have a dramatic effect. There is a fun quiz on the website www.chickmoorman.com, which looks at how phrasing and the way you choose to say things can impact on a child's self-belief.
- For example: 'I'll do it for you', teaches learned helplessness, whereas: 'Let me show you how' is teaching and encourages a child to believe they can do it for themselves after instruction. 'Ask me if you need any help' is correct, as it encourages a child to ask only if they need help; if help is offered before they ask, there is an assumption that they cannot do something themselves. Furthermore, they will never learn to ask for help, which is important part of doing things themselves.
- Choose words that encourage independence and prevent learned helplessness in children. Say to a child:
    - Would you like to talk about some ideas for handling that?
    - Let me show you one example and then you can try.
    - Sounds like you are having a problem. Do you have any ideas how you can fix it?
    - Take a risk and see if you can do it.
    - What kind of things might work to fix this problem? Maybe we can come up with some more together.

Chapter 15: I Can't...

Helplessness can lead to depression later in life, as feelings of worthlessness and inability are compounded. Depressed people tend to see themselves as being at the mercy of their environment rather than in control of it. So it is always worth pointing out to children that their failures are not personal issues or confirmation of their inability. Saying things like 'It is raining, so it will be harder to ride your bike', or, 'This is a particularly difficult puzzle and even big children sometimes have trouble completing it', helps children find external rather than internal causes for disappointment or failure.

It does not mean they cannot carry on trying, but it does mean that it is not so personal. There are always other factors to consider. This does not mean shifting the blame or finding excuses – it means merely providing evidence that we can't always control things!

Self-esteem

Much has been written about self-esteem over the last few years, and the result has been an over-emphasis on praising children regardless of effort or outcome. Some children thrive, with an inflated view of their own capabilities. Others are canny enough to realise that the praise they are being given is, in fact, not a reflection of their abilities or their success rate, and become frustrated into helplessness.

The best way to develop true self-esteem, confidence and pride is to develop appropriate responses to a child's successful and unsuccessful activities. So it is correct to praise a child's ability when he succeeds, but not when he fails. Even young children quickly become familiar with the idea that failure cannot mean that they are good at something. What needs to be emphasised is the potential for being good at something – through effort. Encouragement, not praise, will help a helpless child to develop self-belief and a little get-up-and-go. True self-esteem is self-respect and belief, not a false sense of one's own worth.

Learned helplessness can be a short-term problem in children who have suffered a few knocks and failures, and who have lost confidence in their own ability. It is not a serious issue unless it becomes learned behaviour – a feature of the way that children see their world and their own capabilities. In the long term, it can cause learning difficulties and problems with self-esteem which lead to depressions. By changing the way you speak to children, focussing ability when there are successes and effort when there are failures, you can teach children to believe in themselves again. Simply re-phrasing offers of help or explanations can help a learned helpless child to try something he would not normally attempt.

Key points

- Learned helplessness can be serious in the long term.
- A child who has learned to be helpless needs to believe in himself, not through undirected praise or unmerited successes, but through genuine achievement.
- Teachers and parents need to change the way they speak to a helpless child, to encourage him to think and act for himself.
- Successes should be attributed to ability, while failures should be attributed to effort (or lack of effort).

Chapter 16

Jealousy

Like all emotions, jealousy does not just snap into place. Rather, it emerges through a gradual developmental process in which infants slowly acquire certain kinds of expectations.

All children are capable of experiencing jealousy. In fact, even infants show signs of envy and displeasure when their expectations are not met. Not surprisingly, sibling rivalry can promote the most profound form of jealousy in young children, and even the best-adjusted and well-loved child can regress and lash out when a new baby is born. In some children, however, the problem can escalate out of control, and affect their relationships with friends, family and carers.

In most cases, jealousy in children is purely the result of frustrated expectations. And it is worth looking at jealousy as just that – frustration. Normally, expectations associated with jealousy are specifically related to what psychoanalysts call a 'love object', such as a parent, carer or even a friend. In infants, jealousy is usually a response to a parent directing attention toward a sibling. Firstborn children are upset by this because they develop the expectation of receiving exclusive parental attention.

Later-born children also develop expectations that spark jealousy. Even though they have not received exclusive parental attention, they have enjoyed the special status of being the youngest child in the family and of receiving preferential treatment, because parents tend to give the youngest child the most attention. Through their experiences with parents, infants come to expect parental attention and they expect it to have certain qualities. Happy babies expect it to be plentiful, prompt, predictable and tender.

A new baby

The arrival of a newborn normally means a fairly significant change in a child's environment, and in his routine. Baby paraphernalia is amassed, and preparations often entail changes such as promoting a child from a cot to a bed. Bedrooms might change, a move might be necessary and new routines of attending nursery school or childcare may have been implemented. A child, no matter how young, is keenly aware of changes in his mother's disposition, the presence of new caregivers and slight departures from normal routine. He feels the air fill with the tension of anticipation. These are all stressful for a young child, but do they exacerbate jealousy?

It seems not. Studies show that no matter how structured a child's routine remains, no matter how careful parents are about continuing to supply unwavering attention, jealousy occurs. The reason for this is that it is an innate emotion, and the result of having a rival in the household, whether a new baby is presented as such or not. In this instance, jealousy is about changes in status in a relationship. It is about losing the status of being the only baby or the most important baby in the house.

When parents reduce, or even eliminate, commotion around the newborn's arrival, it still remains a fact that the firstborn child's privileged status is being usurped by a newborn baby. The real source of jealousy is as pronounced as ever. No child who experiences jealousy is necessarily maladjusted, and attributing adult emotions and patterns of behaviour to a child is unfair and unrealistic. Toddlers have not been trained, moulded or socialised to behave politely when they feel jealous. Moreover, the ability to act politely or mask an emotion, requires sophisticated mental tactics, which young children simply do not have. They have no real idea of what is socially acceptable behaviour, nor an awareness of how other people interpret that behaviour. Expecting a toddler to mask his feelings is just not an option. In order for an infant to behave less jealously, he has to actually feel less jealous. Interestingly, research with young siblings shows that the more jealous infants are those who have particularly responsive parents. It seems unfair that more attentive parents are rewarded for their devotion by having more antagonistic infants, but this is only one of the paradoxes of jealousy.

Perverse at it sounds, intense jealousy may simply mean that the infants have come to have great expectations of their parents because they were nurtured so lovingly during early infancy.

A jealous temperament?

All children are different, and respond differently to new situations. A difficult, highly strung child is no more likely to be jealous than a quiet, shy child, but they may have a greater tendency towards jealousy. Temperaments are moulded through socialisation or learning. For example, a large body of research on shyness has shown that children have an inborn tendency to be timid or bold, but this temperament can be channelled via different kinds of life experiences. When a shy, socially timid child is carefully nurtured by patient parents, his shyness can be overcome.

Jealous temperaments can also be channelled. Jealousy can be diminished or it can be intensified. Commonly seen upsurges in acting-up behaviour, aroused by a new baby's arrival, usually subside over a period of time. Warm and playful camaraderie can evolve, sometimes leading to mature and lasting attachments. Yet, in other instances, the problems seem to get worse. Instead of adjustments, antipathies grow and rivalries become only more divisive over time. The way that jealous feelings are dealt with makes all the difference to the eventual outcome.

Other causes of jealousy

Children develop their own routines and objects to which they become attached. When any of these are threatened, they feel frustration, anger and jealousy. If a favourite carer or toy has been usurped by someone else upon arrival at nursery, school or a carer's home, most children will feel undermined, threatened and jealous of the usurper. They may exhibit violence, sulkiness, regressive behaviour, or resort to seeking attention at any cost.

Carers may be bewildered by this reaction, and unaware of the importance placed on a particular routine, person or object by the child. A child's world is small, and his identity and status can be defined by routines and expectations. When these are thwarted, he can become jealous and, through his behaviour, demand that things be returned to normal.

It is important to remember that jealousy is a natural emotion for all human beings, no matter how hard we try to deny it. Children may be jealous of friends, their possessions or their achievements, and they are even more likely to be jealous of siblings who always, in a child's eyes, seem to be getting a better deal. Underpinning most jealousy is dissatisfaction or the misguided belief that the jealous person feels he is not as good as someone else.

How jealousy manifests itself

Sibling rivalry and jealousy are manifested in various, sometimes subtle, ways. Some children are openly hostile to their new siblings, while others are more diffident about expressing their negative feelings. Some older siblings give the baby a good pinch or try to hurt the newborn while your back is turned. Another child may seem to be responding favourably to the new entrant in the family until he politely queries when the baby is being taken back to the hospital. Some older siblings show no animosity to the newborn at all, preferring instead to turn their anger on their mothers. Some children go to another extreme when attempting to suppress their jealousy. They develop a kind of obsession with the newborn. The new baby becomes a point of reference for everything that they see or do. This is neither natural nor healthy.

It is much healthier if your child's hostility is out in the open and he expresses the way he feels. However, do not dwell on it. Acknowledge it and then move on. In the case of children who are suppressing their resentment of the newborn, it may help to draw them out by taking them into confidence and saying that you too get quite annoyed when you have to get up in the middle of the night to feed the baby.

Older children may decide that a new sibling has an easy life, even though it appears to have done nothing to deserve this new status. As a result, they may regress, try out some baby-talk, drink from a bottle, wet the bed, and resort to tantrums and crying for attention. This type of behaviour is normal, and requires patience and understanding. Instead of chastising babyish behaviour, point out the benefits of being older, being a parent's special helper and friend, and praise independent behaviour.

If jealousy is ignored or perceived to be unacceptable, children may just learn to hide it from you, and to lash out when they are not in your presence. They may feel threatened and allow this to carry over into their nursery classes, or with friends. They may feel obliged to make themselves look important in other people's eyes, which can lead to boasting, attention-seeking behaviour, bossiness or even violence. These types of behaviours can cause havoc with other relationships, which is why it is all the more important that you accept a child's feelings and show him ways to channel his normal emotions.

Chapter 16: Jealousy

What parents can do

- Putting a child's feelings into words helps him master them. You can say: 'I know you are angry and jealous, but hurting the baby won't help.'
- Try to put yourself in your child's position. A little empathy can go a long way towards making a child feel understood and valued.
- Look for some good books on the subject, such as *I Feel Jealous*, by Brian Moses (Hodder Wayland), and *Being Jealous*, by Sarah Levete (Copper Beech Books).
- Try not to pay too much attention to a new arrival. Make special times when you are always available for your older child, such as baby's nap time, and remind him how much he is loved and how much you appreciate his company and help with the new baby.
- As long as you reassure a child that he is important and loved, and that your feelings for him have not changed, it will help to ease the blow of having a rival around.
- Identify with your child's concerns. Equally, however, explain what babies need and try to enlist your child's support.
- Try to keep routines as regular as possible, and do not palm older children off with carers and family members instead of offering regular attention. You would be much better off getting someone to watch the baby so that you can spend a little time with your older child, who will be feeling insecure and threatened by the new arrival.
- Find out what each child really feels that he needs and wants, such as more attention or affection, and then take steps towards ensuring that at least some of those needs and desires are met.
- Show equal enthusiasm for all your children's achievements.
- Respect all your children. Every child has the same psychological need to be loved and accepted by his parents, no matter what position he has in the family.

What carers can do

- Try to be understanding and recognise that a child who feels that he has lost his status in his home will try to regain it elsewhere. Help him to feel important by giving him positive ways to shine.
- Ignore any negative behaviour that a child exhibits in order to get attention. He will soon learn that status and importance are not earned by behaving badly.
- Try not to focus too heavily on the birth of a sibling, if this is the cause. A child may feel that the usurper has not only taken over his home but also his friends and carers. Acknowledge the arrival, and ask questions, but try to ensure that routine stays as normal as possible, so that the child feels secure.
- Work on themes of jealousy during story times, drama or playtime. All children benefit from learning that their feelings are normal.
- When jealousy manifests itself as a problem with other children, be firm and consistent with discipline. While it is important to be understanding, relaxing rules will only make a child feel more insecure.
- Recognise that jealousy is normal, and has a variety of different causes. Jealous children are frustrated and feel insecure. Building up their self-esteem, praising their positive

efforts and achievements, and giving them an outset for their frustration will go a long way towards easing their feelings.

Do not assume that your parenting or childcare skills have gone amiss if a child exhibits jealousy. When a child feels that his position or status is threatened, or that his perceived expectations are not being met, jealousy is a normal response. The best and only way to deal with it is to ensure that a child feels loved, that his emotions are acknowledged, that he retains his status in the family, home and childcare facilities, and that his emotional needs are met.

Key points

- Jealousy is a normal emotion experienced by all children at some point in their lives. Even babies experience jealousy when they believe that an important carer or love object has been removed.
- Young children are not emotionally sophisticated enough to hide jealousy.
- Sibling rivalry is a major cause of jealousy in children of all ages. Even careful planning and plenty of attention for older siblings may not be effective, and all parents and carers need to be prepared for that.
- Most young children feel that they have lost status when a new baby arrives on the scene, and they will need reassurance that their importance is not diminished.
- Keeping routines will help to ease the disruption.
- Explaining that jealous feelings are not wrong or bad, and helping children learn to express and channel those feelings, will help them to understand what they are feeling and to develop a more positive self-identity.
- Avoid comparisons, which can spark jealousy in even small children. Pointing out that the new baby is so good and never cries as much as his elder sibling, or comparing the manners of a young friend, will not engender anything but hostility and feelings of inadequacy.

Chapter 17

Lying

Lying is one of the more serious concerns that parents and carers have with regard to children. Is a lying child on course for deviance and dishonesty in later life? Will he grow up to become a manipulative, untrustworthy adult? The good news is that most young children lie for various reasons, many of which are developmental, and it is a habit that is normally outgrown. But outgrowing the lying habit will only occur if parents and carers take the problem in hand, and make clear the importance of honesty.

So why do children lie? First and foremost, you may be surprised to learn that a child's first lessons about lying are normally taught in the home. They hear and pick up those little white lies about not being home when the telephone rings, the enthusiasm shown for disliked gifts and the little secrets partners keep from one another. These all add up in a child's eyes, and make it clear that some lies are acceptable. Social grace and politeness – and even little lies told to avoid rocking the boat – are not concepts that young children understand, and the contradiction between what you say about honesty and what you do yourself can be very confusing.

Furthermore, we actually teach our children to lie to some extent, when we ask them to curb their innate honesty (you don't tell someone you don't like their new haircut, for example, or say you don't like a gift). Most young children do not easily grasp the idea that white lies are different from telling lies that are hurtful.

Creative thinking

A child's creative imagination is often misconstrued as an intentional and purposeful attempt at lying. Pre-schoolers very much enjoy pretend play and making up stories. Young children may blend fantasy into reality through the use of play, primarily because it is fun, but also because it is a form of learning. In essence it is how they learn to become independent adults. They play 'house' or 'Spiderman', and allow their imaginary play to spill over into their real life.

This is not an issue of great concern, and, in fact, offers parents and carers an opportunity to point out the difference between reality and fantasy – encouraging specific time for imaginary play, and becoming involved in television viewing, perhaps, to explain what is real and what is not. It is important to remember that daydreaming and imagination are key parts of who we are, and you do not want to quash that in a child. Being able to pretend we are somewhere else or sometimes even with someone else is often liberating, as well as being stress-releasing.

Avoiding punishment

Another major reason children lie is to escape punishment. Children are primarily motivated by the principles of either pleasure or pain, and while they may gravitate towards that which is enjoyable, it is just as natural for them to avoid that which is not. Consequently, it is worth analysing the form of discipline that you enforce and considering just how severe it is. If you are overly harsh, the more motivated children will be to avoid you when they do wrong.

It is worth noting that children are under a lot of pressure these days – stress, if you like – which is caused by peer pressure (even in the pre-school years), heavily-orchestrated schedules, busy parents and many other demands. Some just cannot keep up with the pressure to perform and may resort to lying to maintain a certain self-image, or to distance themselves from stress in their lives. Some children get into the habit of repetitively lying, because it takes the pressure off. Lying is a habit that is very hard to break.

Other children may lie because they are bored or do not feel that they are receiving adequate attention. Certainly, a child who has gained attention from telling elaborate stories and untruths may continue to do so to maintain parental or social interest. It is worth remembering that children who know the difference between truthfulness and lying may tell elaborate stories that appear believable. They do so in order to create a fantasy or a different existence, which may make them feel more likeable. These children often have a poor self-image and believe that if adults knew the truth about them, they would neither like them nor find them interesting.

Learning values

Children do not have a clear understanding of morals and values, and are only learning the impact of language. They learn that using words can actually change an idea or an event, or portray it in a different way. They may actually begin to believe their own untruths because they sound so much better than the reality, and were so easily concocted and changed.

Children are not just trying to escape consequences or punishment by telling these kinds of lies; they are trying to figure out the place where right turns to wrong and truth turns to untruth. These are normal, healthy questions that children need to answer while they are trying to develop their moral integrity. Understanding them will enable us to respond in ways that help children develop into strong, competent and moral human beings.

Consider too that many children may not have been told the difference between truth and untruth and therefore have not learnt to recognise the difference or the importance.

What you can do

- Children need to learn that lying is wrong, unethical and immoral in most situations. Tell the story about *The Boy Who Cried Wolf* and use it to explain how lying builds distrust. Discuss your beliefs about dishonesty and offer real-life and age-appropriate examples.
- Make it clear to children that the truth is important to you. When children first start testing the limits of the truth, it is important that you tell them that you expect them to tell you the truth, even though it is hard sometimes. Explain to them that the truth is what allows

people to trust one another and that you always want to be able to trust them.

- Be a role model. If children see you lying to a colleague, friend or another child, or undertake any dishonest activity, children will never learn the importance of honesty, and will be terribly confused by your attempt to set them right.
- It may sound contradictory, but it is important to explain the difference between white lies, which are told out of politeness (not to upset granny) and to avoid harm, and malicious, hurtful lies. Most people lie on a daily basis without wishing to cause harm – for example, you may say you are fine when someone enquires about your health, when you are not; you may tell your neighbour that you like her new dress, when you don't. There are certain social niceties that transpire out of respect and mutual kindness that do not always involve the naked truths. Offering your child this information and openly discussing the difference with them may better help them understand the somewhat hypocritical notion of honesty.
- Avoid labelling children as liars. Calling a child names will not shock him into not telling lies. It will make him believe there is something wrong with him, and cause him to lose face. Avoid giving a child a label that he may later feel compelled to live up to.
- Confront children gently but truthfully. When you find that a child has been lying to you, remember that this is an opportunity to both teach about the importance of the truth, and to help them answer some of his underlying questions.
- Angry, punitive responses are more likely to teach children to lie out of fear. Consequently they learn that if they can avoid getting caught, it is acceptable to lie.
- It is important to help a child avoid losing face. Talk about what makes telling the truth difficult – admitting to mistakes, doing things we wish we hadn't, fear of recrimination, concern about how someone will respond, embarrassment, and so on. And explain that these are only temporary feelings, and that the relief of getting things off our chest is a lot better than compounding the problem with a lie that then may (and probably will) be found out.
- Make it easy for children to tell the truth. Praise their honesty, and deal with any misdemeanour which might have led to lying later. Encourage them by telling them that you understand how hard it must have been to tell the truth under the circumstances.
- If a child regularly lies about one part of his life – whether he simply fictionalises his life or something more serious – try to work out what may be causing him stress or distress in that area. If the pressure is relieved, he may not feel the need to escape to an alternative reality, or to create a series of events or a life that does not exist.
- Ensure that children do not get attention only when they lie. Show as much interest in their reality, in what they achieve on a day-to-day basis as you can. If they get plenty of attention for positive behaviour, they will be less likely to lie to attract your interest and notice.
- Work on a child's self-esteem, and make sure he feels good about himself for who he is. If he has a poor self-image, he may feel that he has to invent things to catch your interest, or to make himself more interesting. Again, take steps to notice the little things that make him special. If you catch him telling lies to enhance his self-image, point out the things about him that you like. Show no real interest in the fabrications, and focus instead on the realities.

- Offer children opportunities to make amends. Once you have discovered and discussed a situation with your child, both of you might be able to think of a way to make up for the lie. Saying sorry is one way; but also making up for an act that was supposedly done (lying about brushing teeth or putting toys away, for example, is easily rectified). Furthermore, if the lie involves an act that embarrassed a child (for example wetting his trousers or breaking something), be sensitive to his feelings and suggest positive ways to avoid the problem in the future. If a child feels that you are on his side, he'll be much more likely to be honest and to come to you with problems in the future.
- Before children can distinguish whether or not they have been truthful, they need to witness the difference between what is real and what is unreal. Young children will need to be taught this on a variety of occasions, which makes books and television good learning tools. Discussing dreams after sleep time is another great example for children to learn from.

Overall, dealing with a child who does not tell the truth is difficult and can be frustrating. Be sure to teach a child the importance of trust in relationships, including the trust they should have in themselves. Avoid putting a child in situations where deceit or exaggerations can occur (such as highly competitive sports) and do not blame a child for lying unless you have determined for sure that they are responsible for the situation.

Have any discussion involving dishonesty privately and do not make children afraid of telling the truth. Always seek an underlying reason for why a child felt compelled to lie, and try to address those reasons. Above all, remember that much pre-school lying is simply experimental and a part of normal development, and does not set a child on a course for a life of crime.

Key points

- Almost all children lie to some extent in the pre-school years, as they learn to use language, experiment with independence and define themselves.
- Much lying has to do with difficulty understanding the difference between fantasy and reality.
- Some children lie for attention, so be sure not to give attention for negative behaviour.
- Make sure children feel good about themselves and develop a positive self-image, so that they do not feel that it is necessary to be someone or something else through a series of lies.
- Remember that lying is a habit that is hard to break. You will need to be firm but understanding.
- Lying gives parents and carers a chance to teach moral values and the importance of trust in relationships.

Chapter 18

My Way or No Way!

For most parents and carers, the years between the terrible twos and pre-school can be challenging and often exasperating. As toddlers begin to assert their authority, find their independence and test the world around them, they become defiant, and the word 'no' is often the mainstay of their vocabularies. As difficult as this can be to manage, defiance in this age group is completely natural. However, without pro-active parenting, regular routines and discipline, as well as a firm set of boundaries, some children never outgrow their defiance, and can develop what is known as a conduct disorder. As frustrating as it may become, this stage of childhood requires firm parenting and a clear set of expectations, accompanied by a good sense of humour.

As any parent or carer of a two-year-old knows, not only do young children do the very things they are asked not to do – and on a regular basis – but they often refuse to do them *because* they've been asked to. A clear set of instructions is met with 'no', and in many cases the complete opposite of the desired behaviour is achieved. I know this from experience, too. As the mother of an active 20-month-old son, I was aghast, just yesterday, when my middle son said: 'No, don't throw the ball out of the car window' to his younger brother. Why? Because I knew that the ball would go straight out of the window, and it did. Give a toddler a set of instructions, particularly in a firm tone of voice, and you can expect the opposite to happen.

Now herein lies the theory of reverse psychology, which so many parents and carers adopt with little ones. It works because children believe they are doing what *they* want and not what *you* want. The basis for this is, of course, the fact that children challenge everything, as soon as they realise they are able to – and if they feel cornered, powerless or challenged themselves, they immediately assert their will and give a good attempt at showing just who *is* boss in the household.

Why is defiance natural?

If it seems as if the toddler or pre-schooler in your care is intentionally disobeying you, or disregarding your wishes, you are right. They are, and it is exactly that: intentional.

Several studies have indicated why this happens. According to most current psychological thought, children are, at this stage, learning what happens when people want different things. In other words, they are learning about conflict and are using a powerful learning mechanism — hypothesis testing. The terrible twos are really just a part of children's experimental programme to figure out the world. Primary caregivers, unfortunately, are the main test subjects.

By the age of two, children are trying to understand conflict. At younger ages, children believe that their desires (what they want, what they like) are the same as everyone else's desires. When everyone wants and likes the same things, there's no real conflict. But at around 18 months, children begin to understand an important new concept — people have different desires.

One creative experiment, undertaken in 1997, and reported by the Talaris Research Institute, used biscuits and broccoli to provide this evidence. Researchers showed 14-month-old and 18-month-old children two different bowls of food—one filled with Goldfish biscuits and one filled with raw broccoli. When given the choice between the two foods, both the 14-month-old and 18-month-old children chose the biscuit.

Next, a researcher tasted the foods in front of the babies. When she ate the crackers, she made a disgusted face and said 'Yuck'. With the broccoli, she smiled and said 'Yum'. Then, with both bowls of food in front of her, she put out her hands and asked the babies to give her some food. This was the experimental question: would the babies give her some biscuits or some broccoli?

The 14-month-old babies gave the researcher biscuits, even though she said 'yuck' when she ate them before. They didn't yet understand how another person could want or prefer something different from their own tastes and desires.

The 18-month-old babies gave the researcher broccoli, showing that despite their own preference for biscuits, they understood that the adult preferred the vegetable. They understood that the adult had different desires for food.

In other words, 18-month-old children are beginning to understand that people are truly different, and that what they want is not necessarily what adults want. And this is a recipe for conflict. Children need to learn how conflict works — and how to resolve it.

Hypothesis testing and conflict

To learn about conflict, 2 year-old toddlers launch a series of experiments. This process is called hypothesis testing, and it is a powerful way children (and scientists) learn about the world. It starts with what children already know about people and their desires. With this knowledge, children make predictions (hypotheses) and test them to see if their ideas are correct.

Hypothesis testing involves 5 steps:

1. Making observations
2. Asking questions
3. Creating hypotheses (what they think will happen based on what they know)
4. Testing hypotheses
5. Evaluating the evidence

So in your household, your two-year-old sees that you want him to eat his breakfast. He knows you do. He really doesn't want to eat it, because it isn't what he had in mind – and perhaps not the same as what someone else is eating. He knows you won't like it if he doesn't eat it – and he also wonders how you will react if he throws it on the floor.

Here's what hypothesis testing might look like:

1. I don't want to eat my breakfast and I want to throw it on the floor. I know that my mother doesn't want me to do this (observation).
2. What will happen if I do throw it on the floor (question)?
3. When I threw my dinner on the floor last night, my mother was angry. She will probably get angry again (hypothesis).
4. I will throw it on the floor, even though my mother looks angry (testing).
5. She is very angry – and this is what happens when she is angry (evaluating the evidence).

This is, of course, a very simplistic version of what goes on with a toddler, and in a toddler's mind, and does not take into consideration the tantrums, the quick reactions, and intense emotions; however, the basis is that children are naturally motivated to learn more about how conflict works and how it gets resolved.

Is that it?

Of course not! This is one element of a child's defiance. There are many more:

- Children who are learning to become independent have a natural wish to assert that independence and a belief that their views and wishes are more important than others'. Children of this age are only beginning to learn the concept of compassion and are not even near selflessness. So when given the opportunity, they will take steps to ensure that their needs are met and that you are aware of their importance. No matter what.
- While firm parenting and discipline are important at this age, some carers are a little too firm and use the word 'no' a little too often. Children who always hear the word 'no' for everything new they attempt will naturally become more confrontational – largely because they feel powerless and have little choice. They may also learn that using 'no' is the only way to get what they want – much as you do.
- Along with self-interest comes the continued development of toddlers' emotions, such as anger and frustration - which mainly appear in the form of rage and defiance. It is not unusual for them to express anger and frustration by hitting, kicking, shoving, or biting. Learning to recognise these emotions, connect them to their behaviour, and to gain control over that behaviour is an ongoing process. It isn't learned overnight, and they often, simply because they don't *understand* how they feel, lash out, become defiant and over-emotional. Much defiance stems from frustration and a lack of self-control, which is, ultimately, learned.
- Language is another important factor to consider in understanding behaviour at this age. While this is a period of tremendous growth in expressive language, not all toddlers are as verbally skilled as others at this age. Some may not yet have the words they need to express their feelings and frustrations. Others may have the words, but are not yet able to

connect the feelings and behaviours they experience. If you ask them to do something that makes them unhappy, they simply feel unhappy – and become defiant or angry. They don't understand that unhappiness can have other outlets – they just let loose.

- Parents and carers, not surprisingly, have expectations for certain behaviours – it's part of the parenting process, and guiding children about what is acceptable and what is not. However, just as a child leaves babyhood and begins to develop a sense of self, parents begin to teach new rules to them – when they can shout, when they should use the potty, what they have to wear, what they have to eat, and much, much more. So at the same time that a child's expanding capabilities require parents to begin to teach the child self-control and self-restraint, the child has developed a new and powerful sense of self and begins to assert his will quite insistently. Not surprisingly, this leads to tension and power struggles.

What can you do?

- Make sure your expectations are appropriate for your child – if they are unrealistic or too high, your child will struggle to meet them and defy you rather than even try.
- Consider your child's temperament when choosing your discipline method. A highly strung, defiant child will not respond to overly harsh parenting and you will lock horns repeatedly. Much better, in this case, to outline expectations early, offer praise and rewards for the type of behaviour you want to see, and plenty of choices (see below), so that your tiger doesn't feel caged.
- Understand that children need to learn about conflict from their parents and caregivers. These young children aren't bad, they're curious. Expect them to test you often.
- Provide consistent responses. When children test their hypotheses, they are gathering evidence about how people deal with conflict. The best evidence is reliable, consistent and loving.
- Focus on the positive aspects of this age. These toddlers are not only learning how conflict happens, but how conflict gets resolved. If they are surrounded with healthy, consistent models, children can learn how to handle future disagreements in constructive and effective ways.
- Always build on the positives, give the child praise and positive reinforcement when he shows flexibility or co-operation.
- Choose your battles. Prioritise the things you want your child to do. If you say no and argue constantly, he will learn nothing apart from the fact that conflict is a part of life and that he has his own role to play – protecting himself and his newfound will.
- Set up reasonable, age-appropriate limits with consequences that can be enforced consistently.
- Help toddlers identify their feelings and label them with words such as angry, upset, happy, and sad. If they are becoming defiant out of frustration, understanding how they are feeling is the first step towards negotiation – and, indeed, understanding how other people feel as well.
- Offer a variety of strategies that the toddler can use in frustrating situations, especially words, gestures and asking for help.

- Offer choices. Offering a limited choice can be exhausting, but it is the best way to avoid a showdown. Do you want to wear your pink tights or your blue ones? Would you like your juice in the red cup or the yellow one? Do you want your story before your bath or after? This doesn't change the rules in the sense that the tights are worn, the juice is drunk and the bath takes place, but a child feels as if he has some control of his environment. This also offers the *appearance* of options, when there aren't really any.
- Teach your toddler other responses. One of the reasons toddlers say 'no' so much is they don't know very many words. Help your child expand his vocabulary – try teaching 'maybe', 'sometimes', 'maybe later', 'not right now', 'no thank you' and even 'YES'. And model this yourself. If you always say 'no', your child will probably do the same.
- Instead of greeting a 'no' with a firm response – suggest an alternative. 'Oh, do you mean not right now?', 'Oh, maybe after tea, then?', 'You don't like those socks? OK, I'll wear them!'. Humour can go a long way and teach children that 'no' isn't the only option if they don't want to do something.
- Similarly, use different words from 'no' when you want to control or divert behaviour – for example 'It's not safe to do that', 'We don't hit the kitten because it makes her sad' or 'We don't throw the ball out of the window because we will lose it'. Save 'no' for safety issues.
- Diversion is probably the best technique available to all parents and carers – sense a battle on the horizon, or a storm brewing? Move rooms or activities, and change tacks. One of the nicest things about little ones is that they have short memories, and easily forget their angry feelings when something new approaches.
- Remember that young children grow and develop so quickly that they are often bewildered by their changing world – and the control they seem to have over it. Testing often involves a search for security – are my boundaries still there? How far can I go? Is the response always the same? Children become much more secure when they are dealt with in a consistent fashion, and they know the ropes. This also involves expectations – make sure your child knows what you expect, never assume. Set the boundaries, make them clear, and be consistent. The same boundaries may be tested several times but if the response is the same, your child will eventually move on.
- Finally, make your day and your lifestyle as routine as possible. If you *always* clear up the toys after play, *always* wash your hands after using the loo, *always* get dressed after breakfast and *always* turn off the telly before dinner, your child will become accustomed to his world and his role in it. Again, children feel much more secure when they know what is expected of them, and what comes next. You are much less likely to engage in a battle if behaviour becomes second nature through regular routines.

Oppositional defiant disorder

Oppositional behaviour is often a normal part of development for two- to three- year-olds and early adolescents. However, openly uncooperative and hostile behaviour becomes a serious concern when it is so frequent and consistent that it stands out when compared to behaviour of other children of the same age and developmental level, and when it affects the child's social, family, and academic life.

Chapter 18: My Way or No Way!

In children with Oppositional Defiant Disorder (ODD), there is an ongoing pattern of uncooperative, defiant and hostile behaviour toward authority figures which seriously interferes with the youngster's day-to-day functioning. Symptoms of ODD may include:

- frequent temper tantrums
- excessive arguing with adults
- active defiance and refusal to comply with adult requests and rules
- deliberate attempts to annoy or upset people
- blaming others for mistakes or misbehaviour
- often being touchy or easily annoyed by others
- frequent anger and resentment
- mean and hateful talking when upset
- seeking revenge

Five to fifteen percent of all school-age children have ODD. The causes of ODD are unknown, but many parents report that their child with ODD was more rigid and demanding than the child's siblings from an early age.

If any of these symptoms seem familiar to you, it's important that you have your child assessed – there may be learning difficulties, mood or anxiety disorders or hyperactive problems at the root, which are causing the behaviour. There is plenty of help available, so see your GP or health visitor to arrange an assessment.

As difficult as it may be to face the demands of a defiant youngster, with a little pre-planning, regular routines, outlined expectations and consistent discipline, your child will eventually learn what is expected of him, and realise that he can exert his will and use his independence in other ways. Part of this has to do with offering choices, and allowing a little natural experimentation; all children do it, and it's entirely natural. But a consistent response goes a long way towards teaching children that there are other ways to express themselves, that they do have some power over their environments, and that there are options to the word 'no'. In some children, defiance becomes a conduct disorder. All parents and carers should be aware of this, and watch for the signs.

Key points

- Defiance in children is part of the developmental process, and involves something known as hypothesis testing.
- As children learn to assert their independence, they will push boundaries and make unreasonable demands. Responding consistently will ensure that they learn the appropriate lessons and become more secure.
- Discipline and consistency are the most important elements of dealing with defiance, and so are realistic expectations. But offer choices so that your child does not lash out through feelings of powerlessness.
- In the vast majority of cases, defiance is outgrown – in fact, it can literally disappear overnight.

Chapter 19

Potty Problems

As a prerequisite for joining many early years settings, most children must be potty-trained. However, with school starting earlier and earlier in many boroughs, training must often take place before a child is actually ready, leading to regular accidents, emotional problems and potty resistance. Even older children experience accidents and can regress, even when training appears to have been established. The important thing to remember is that all children are eventually trained, and unless there are serious emotional or physical problems, it is a hurdle which can be addressed with a little common sense and empathy.

Potty-training, whether undertaken by a childminder, parent or other carer, is not a laborious process, but it does demand some patience and planning. Getting it right the first time round does mean fewer setbacks, and it eliminates the chances of problems cropping up at a later date. Everyone has their own tried and tested means by which they teach their children to use a potty, and as long as parents and carers are consistent, patient and positive, it should be a fairly painless procedure. The most important thing, however, is timing. A child who is potty-trained at a young age (prior to two) is not more advanced or clever than his peers, nor will he benefit in any way from learning early. In fact, studies show that children who are trained too early are much more likely to experience problems and to regress than children who are trained at the appropriate time.

When to train?

Physical and emotional development are occurring at the same time and influence each other. Natural stages of emotional and physical mastery build on each other and are best experienced sequentially in the naturally occurring readiness of a child. The natural period of time in which consistent interest in toilet training occurs is usually between two and three years of age. It is at this age that children have already mastered some sense of accomplishment from being able to successfully manipulate their environment in many ways. They can go and get a toy for themselves, reach out to pet a cat, pull a book off a shelf, build a tower and use language to get what they want. It is from this cumulative experience that the confidence to master toilet training emerges.

Self-regulation is an enormous achievement because the child is aware of the accomplishment. Early toilet training often results in regression later on, which the child may experience as a sense of shame or failure, rather than pride and confidence. For some children, playing with a potty or observing others may be interesting and the source of great curiosity, and even experimentation, in younger children. Children as young as 16 months may attempt the feat of using a potty themselves, or express an interest in going without nappies. However, although there is nothing wrong with allowing a child to experiment at this age, it is a mistake to consider it the beginning of full training. It may serve as a kind of preparation for later toilet training, but it will not result in successful control of the release of complex sphincter muscles, which are largely involuntary.

A period of development

Remember that a child under the age of two is too young to consistently be aware of his bodily functions. He is too busy mastering the voluntary muscles involved in walking to even consider the nuances of controlling involuntary processes. It would be overloading a toddler's system to introduce an additional developmental challenge, especially one which he cannot successfully achieve. This could even cause delays in other areas of development that are primed for this time.

Secondly, an expectation to perform (even mildly) on the potty at this period in development could result in feelings of failure, inadequacy or general stress associated with toilet training. Early pressure could put paid to the emotional sense of pride that coincides with successful toilet training later. A child could miss out on the sense of mastery which is such a critical part of this developmental milestone when it occurs at the appropriate time.

It is often the case that children regress in one area of development when progressing in another. For example, research shows that when children challenge themselves to learn to read, it is helpful if they have something to return to intermittently that was mastered earlier (such as building blocks). It is thought that this gives them a period of rest to assimilate new information and that the return to something mastered lends confidence to the ability to learn something new.

A period of developmental challenge in one area of a child's life (starting school, attending playgroup, learning to paint, identify letters, use a jungle gym or swim, for example) may put pressure on an earlier part of his development which was weakly established.

So if a child learns to use the toilet too early, regression is a common feature whenever there is a new developmental challenge. And it is worth remembering that the years between two and five are some of the most demanding on both an emotional and a physical level for all children.

What causes problems?

It is clear that training too early is often a feature of most setbacks, and the rush to get a child out of nappies in advance of nursery places or other school-like environments can put pressure on even the most confident and accomplished child. There are, however, other reasons why children have accidents, or refuse to be trained. These include:

- Using toilet training as an attention-seeking device. Many children cotton on to the fact that having accidents guarantees attention, even if it is negative, and continue as a means to get that attention. Even in a busy nursery or childcare environment, it is a pretty neat way of ensuring that a teacher or carer offers their full attention.

- Stress in one area of a child's life can lead to regression in other parts, partly because they want the comfort of being baby-like and dependent again, and partly because the concentration it takes to master and continue to be successfully trained is not available.
- Being genuinely frightened about sitting on a potty or an unfamiliar toilet, or negotiating a different loo.
- Inconsistent training, particularly among different caregivers.
- Painful bowel movements from being constipated (see below), which makes the experience frightening.
- Being stubborn – some children are locked in a power struggle with a parent or carer, something that is very common as children become independent. Using control over where and how he has a bowel movement or urinates is one way of exerting independence and showing rebellion.
- Allergies. Lactose intolerance (the inability to digest milk or milk products) is the most common, but other foods can cause allergies, too. Common side-effects are bowel problems, which may be affecting training.
- Urinary infections. These include pain or burning sensations while urinating, straining to urinate, colour changes in the urine, foul-smelling urine, frequent urination that produces very little, or a split stream of urine. Other signs could be abdominal pain or a fever of an undetermined origin. Such infections are not uncommon in small children, and can undermine even the best toilet habits. Even after a urinary problem has cleared up, a child may still remember and fear the pain of urinating, and this may complicate potty-training.
- Constipation may be preventing a child from wanting to move his bowels, because it is painful. Chronic constipation can put pressure on the bladder and cause daytime, as well as night-time, accidents. Increasing both the fibre content of your child's diet as well as fluid intake should help a lot – that means plenty of whole grains, and fresh fruit and vegetables.
- Interference from others. Siblings can set a child off by playing on fears and expectations; friends or even teachers may say the wrong thing. If a child is embarrassed about potty-training, or develops negative connotations with anything it involves, chances are there will be problems.

What can you do?

Carers and teachers

- Make sure that you show a child an unfamiliar loo, and how it works. Children can be daunted by even the smallest differences.
- Some children will need the reassurance of a potty or their own potty seat. Speak to parents about bringing the chair or seat along, or sending in a duplicate.
- Do not hesitate to remind children about using the loo – children are easily distracted, and at a time of vast developmental change, they are simply not equipped to take and keep everything on board.
- Watch out for signs of stress. A child under pressure may regress. It may help to talk to parents about anything that might be going on at home, so that you are aware of problems that may be hampering training.

- Ask the child to show you how he would toilet train a doll or cuddly toy. Watch the child's behaviour and listen carefully to commands and instructions. If the child uses abusive language, scolds and handles the toy roughly, it might be a clue that your own or someone else's attitudes and actions are at fault. Show him the right way to do it by being patient and kind.
- Perhaps ask a child to draw a picture of the loo. Ask for explanations of anything you do not understand. You may get some clues about worries or fears the child has been repressing.
- Put a star chart outside the door to the loo, and encourage all children to stick up a star when they have used it. It takes attention away from those having accidents, and gives all children an opportunity to feel proud of their achievements.
- Choose books about potty-training for story sessions and engage children in a discussion afterwards. All children feel better if they know that what they are experiencing is normal, and that problems do not have to be hidden. Good suggestions include *A Potty for Me!* by Karen Katz, *Once Upon a Potty*, by Alona Frankel, *I Want My Potty!* by Tony Ross and *Potty Poo-Poo Wee-Wee* by Colin McNaughton.
- Deal with accidents in a calm way, avoiding drawing unnecessary attention to the event or the child.
- If you suspect that accidents are attention-seeking, be sure to offer plenty of attention for positive behaviour, so that children do not feel the need to get your attention in other ways.
- Encourage a child to become involved in cleaning and changing himself after accidents. He will need your help, but you will show a child that you respect his independence and trust his ability to deal with the problem himself, which helps to bolster self-esteem.
- If a child has clearly been trained too quickly or too early, talk to his parents about slowing down for a while. Pushing a child who is not ready will only lead to problems. Good signs of readiness include interest in using the potty or toilet, a series of dry nappies throughout the day and after naps, is able to walk well (to get to the loo or potty!), can pull up a nappy or pants and can understand the concept of using a potty. If the pressure is off, a child will have some space to get used to other demands on his time and energy, and be much more receptive to the idea of being like other children under these circumstances. It may be difficult to keep tabs on a youngster in nappies, but it will do his confidence good if he feels that he can be successful at his attempt, rather than constantly having accidents.

Parents

While most children show signs of physical readiness to begin using the toilet as toddlers, usually between two and three years of age, not all children have the intellectual or psychological readiness to be potty-trained at this age. Be sure to go at your child's pace and show strong encouragement and praise when he is successful. Even after he begins to use the potty, it is normal to have accidents and for him to regress or relapse at times and refuse to use the potty. The process of being fully potty- trained can take time, often up to three to six months for most children. Having accidents or occasionally refusing to use the the potty is normal and not considered resistance.

If you do meet resistance, consider the following:

- Do not underestimate the importance of talking to your child and explaining what happens. Many parents train a child without explaining expectations, which leads to confusion.
- Make potty-training a significant event when you explain why he is ready, what will happen next, and celebrate with a set of underpants. Most children find it easier to go without nappies during both day and night, so when the box is finished, make it clear to your child that he does not need them any more either at night or during the day. If they are used part-time, it can be difficult for a child to learn full control. And if they are there for emergencies, you can bet that one will arise. Better to deal calmly with accidents, and show faith in his ability to get it right.
- If you do have a child who refuses to have a bowel movement other than in a nappy, limit this activity to the loo. This is not always possible, but is easy if he always asks for a nappy just to have a bowel movement. Next, have him sit on the potty to have a bowel movement, even if he continues to wear his nappy. Then work on getting his nappy off by opening it and eventually taking it off. During this process, you should give lots of praise and rewards during each step.
- If he is having a hard time learning to use the potty, but isn't necessarily resistant to the idea, then developing a regular daily routine of sitting on the potty for five or ten minutes every few hours may be helpful.
- Most importantly, avoid physical punishment for not using the potty, even in an older child. It can be appropriate to verbally let him know that you disapprove of his not using the potty, but this should not get to the point of yelling, shaming or nagging.
- If he is resistant, do not offer him opportunities to say 'no'. Say 'It's time to try' rather than 'Do you have to go?'
- Personalise a potty seat with stickers or anything else that makes the seat his own.
- Watch your child's diet and ensure that he gets plenty of fresh, whole foods that will prevent constipation. Sitting with a child while he is attempting a bowel movement can be reassuring and take the pressure off.
- Consider physical problems that might be affecting his ability to be trained. If you are worried, pay a visit to your GP, who can rule out anything serious.
- Remember to start well in advance of beginning nursery or at a childminder's. With all the change afoot, he is likely to have more accidents than he normally would. You want a good six months under your belt, with at least a month of complete success, before he is ready to be trusted alone. If that means putting off a nursery place for half a term, so be it. Not all children are ready at the same time, and rushing it is a recipe for problems in the future.

Many potty problems are simply the result of pushing a child when he is not ready. Emotional and physical development takes place at great speed during the toddler and pre-school years, and one task must be mastered before another is attempted. Expecting a child to be toilet-trained at the same time that he starts school or takes on another challenging task is unrealistic.

Chapter 19: Potty Problems

The majority of children will suffer setbacks during and after training, during periods of stress, developmental changes or even when they simply feel the need for more attention. The solution is always to pay close attention to successes, and to overlook – or deal calmly with – problems and accidents.

Key points

- During periods of change, potty-training should be put on the back burner.
- If resistance sets in, it is best to take a step back and to begin again in a few weeks' or months' time, even if that means putting off a nursery place for a while.
- Children need to master one stage of development before they are able to succeed at another. Take things slowly, and do not expect a child to go through periods of change or to learn new things, without setbacks along the way.
- Take time to explain your expectations, and what a child needs to do. A helping hand and a little reassurance may be all a child needs to get to grips with a new situation.

Chapter 20

Regression

Reverting to thumb-sucking, potty-training accidents and a dependence upon comfort toys are all classic regressive behaviours which commonly occur in young children. But do not dismiss the problem as simply being attention-seeking. Regression occurs for a variety of different reasons, and children who exhibit this behaviour are more often than not showing signs of stress.

Sigmund Freud described several mechanisms which children may use to defend themselves against the anxieties or uncertainties of growing up. A child who experiences too much anxiety or too many conflicts at any stage of development may retreat to an earlier, less traumatic stage. Such developmental reversals are examples of a defence mechanism that Freud called regression.

Even a well-adjusted adult may regress from time to time in order to forget problems or reduce anxiety and children, who are less likely to think through and overcome emotional difficulties, are even more likely to revert to behaviours that they associate with comfort and care.

In pre-school children, something as simple as a family row may cause feelings of panic and anxiety which manifest themselves as regressive behaviours. And perfectly normal children experience fears, which they are unable to explain or quantify. Fear of animals, the dark or monsters are all common in pre-schoolers, and because they cannot actually work out why they are frightened or rationalise their fears, children often internalise them, which compounds regression.

Separation anxiety is also a common cause of regression, and children who are starting a new nursery or playgroup, changing carers or even experiencing a change in routine, may suddenly become clingy and more baby-like. It is also important to remember that there may be problems at home – divorce, a new baby, marital problems, or even violence or abuse – driving the regression. As a teacher or carer, your role is not to play detective, but any serious concerns should be reported.

Two steps forward…

Children's development is not linear or even. Often children take a few steps forward and several back. When a child first learns a new skill, like weaning, using the toilet independently or spending the night away from home, he often regresses in other areas, forgetting already established skills.

Child development theorist Jean Piaget coined the word 'disequilibrium' to describe the out-of-balance times children often go through just before they learn something new. Children who are on the verge of crawling sometimes get fussy or start waking at night. Children who are just about to work out how to play successfully with other children may become unusually aggressive. In other words, regression may well be a sign of a developmental leap, of which there are many in the pre-school years. It helps teachers and carers to know that children's struggles are indicative of their attempts to grow and therefore to provide appropriate support.

Encouraging emotional development

One thing that teachers and carers can do to address regressive behaviours is to teach children an emotional vocabulary. This will enable them to verbalise their emotions and get them off their chest, an incredibly important skill for all children to learn, and one that they will use throughout their lives as they face and learn to cope with stress and anxiety.

And do not underestimate the possibility that young children can experience stress. An American study found, for example, that even babies left to cry experience the physical effects of stress (raised cortisone levels, for example), with significant physiological changes to their bodies. Vivian Hill, director of professional educational psychology training at the Institute of Education, London, says that a survey of a hundred primary schools across the country showed that teachers believe many children are affected by stress. One in eight was seriously stressed, becoming clingy, vomiting, losing bladder control and displaying regressive behaviour.

Physical manifestation of emotional problems is very common in young children, which is why it is even more important to give them the tools to express themselves. One way to do this is to operate a regular circle time in your classroom or nursery group, where children can talk about feelings. Suggest a topic or read a story about a child with a problem (being afraid of the dark, for example, or not wanting to go to school, or even the birth of a new sibling), and then ask the children how they would feel if they were that child. This works on a one-to-one basis as well. Start off by helping to provide the children with words, such as 'angry', 'jealous', 'hurt' or 'sad' and give them free rein to add their own. Choose a variety of different situations, so that most children will identify with at least one.

Encourage children to draw or paint emotions. It may sound odd, but asking children to draw 'hot and tired', 'angry' or 'happy' is one way of encouraging them to examine an emotion and then express it. Use their artwork as a springboard for further discussions. For example, 'what makes you angry or frightened?'.

Dealing with change

A new carer, playgroup, teacher or class can make a child feel frightened and insecure, even if he does not obviously exhibit any anxiety. There are many things teachers and carers can do to help make transitions easier.

- Many nurseries and playgroups discourage comfort toys, but they can be used for a short period of time in order to help a child to adjust. Transitional comfort objects, such as a 'blankie' which a child consistently uses to feel comfortable when in an unfamiliar setting, should be permitted when needed to make a successful transition into a new environment.

- Other children should be encouraged to be empathetic and respectful of a child using a transitional object and support a new child in adjusting. These transitional objects generally find their way to the cloakroom or a box by the front door, and can eventually stay at home fairly quickly.
- A child's need for a comfort toy diminishes with the development of secure attachments to new people. Safe, protective environments help children feel secure and willing to take risks with unfamiliar people and situations. Make sure you are warm and welcoming but not overwhelming.
- Establish predictable routines that help children anticipate activities and events. Provide interesting and attractive materials and equipment which encourage involvement in your environment. Allow children time to observe and move slowly toward interactions with people and materials. And never use a comfort toy as a punishment or reward for behaviour.
- With increasing intellectual and emotional maturity, children are able to use memory instead of a holey blanket or tattered stuffed animal to help cement their attachments to home and family. Demonstrate your respect for children's struggles with dependence and independence – their need for the familiar and secure battling with the need for skill, mastery and knowledge.

Overcoming anxieties

Carers and teachers can make change easier for children by:

- developing and participating in rituals for parents' departures
- helping parents to understand that comfort toys are important to most pre-schoolers and are, in fact, a sign of increasing emotional and intellectual maturity
- encouraging all children to bring a comfort toy from home
- showing children where to keep a comfort toy when it is not in use
- teaching the children to respect the comfort toy as special property (something not likely to be shared)
- helping children to find security in your attention and routines, gradually diminishing their need for 'home' comforts.

Addressing the problem

- Most children will revert to age-appropriate behaviour when they feel more secure. Although you may find thumb-sucking irritating or toilet accidents disruptive, it is important to remain calm and not draw attention to the problem. If a child learns that the only way he gets attention from a teacher or carer is by behaving like a baby, normal and situational regression may become a longer-term problem. Instead, focus on praising and encouraging more grown-up or responsible behaviours, and calmly deal with any accidents without fuss.
- Create a warm, trusting atmosphere that encourages the expression of positive and negative emotions.
- Remember that small children, in particular those at pre-school age, find fear to be incomprehensible; the risk is, since the child does not know how to define fear, that he

can become isolated and close himself into a world of solitude.
- Encourage the expression of emotion, not just by verbal discussion but by using expressive methods such as drawings, games, music and theatre. The best instruments to use with pre-school children are drawings, fairy tales, nursery rhymes and little dramas with toys or puppets. Dramatisation, and consequent identification, allows the child to express his feelings and fears easily. A child at this age may have problems communicating, and perhaps may not confide in others for fear of being called a coward.

Something more serious

If a child fails to respond to a secure environment with lots of encouragement and regular routine after a few weeks, there may be something more serious afoot, and you will need to address your concerns to parents or even the authorities. You may find yourself the recipient of a child's disclosure, and you must deal with this sensitively.

Children generally disclose with great hesitation and often with feelings of fear and guilt. Frequently they only hint or tell a bit of the story to see how a teacher or carer reacts before fully disclosing. For this reason it is important to remain calm and supportive, and avoid showing either verbally or non-verbally any feelings that might make the child regret having confessed or divulged a problem.

Most regressive behaviour is completely natural, and a part of the developmental process. It normally occurs when a child is under pressure, or experiencing stress or anxiety in one or more areas. Teachers and carers can help children to adapt to stressful situations and to deal with their anxiety by providing a caring, supportive environment, with plenty of discussion about emotions and feelings and a regular routine. Keeping up communication with parents is also very important, to establish if there is something at home driving the behaviour. However irksome or distressing regressive behaviour may be, it almost always resolves itself in a few short weeks.

Key points

- Regression in children often occurs before a developmental link, or as a response to stress or anxiety.
- Teachers and carers can help children by creating a regular routine and encouraging the expression of emotions.
- It is important to allow regressive behaviours, such as the need for a comfort toy, to be expressed. Comfort toys are good transitional tools.
- Children should never be made to feel silly or babyish for regression. Calmly accept their behaviour as a transitional stage. Focus attention and praise on behaviour that is more responsible, independent and age-appropriate.
- Parents should be aware of your routines, and encouraged to explain their own, in order to help children settle more quickly.
- In rare cases, regression can be a sign of a serious problem at home. Teachers and carers must be aware of procedures for reporting problems, and dealing with disclosure by children.

Chapter 21

Self-respect

Self-esteem is something that all carers, parents and teachers try to instil in children, to give them confidence, a healthy self-image and all-important self-belief. But has the self-esteem train gone off the rails? The over-focus on praising children has led to some fairly unholy monsters, showing little regard for others and confidence based on false adulation rather than justified achievement, effort or worth. Most importantly, perhaps, many children today have little respect – and this boils down to the fact that they have no real respect for themselves.

A child might have high self-esteem, but if he does not respect himself, he will never respect others. So what is more important, self-respect or self-esteem, and how can you get little ones on track?

Self-esteem can also be defined as the combination of feelings of capability with feelings of being loved. A child who is happy with his achievements but does not feel loved may eventually experience low self-esteem. Likewise, a child who feels loved but is hesitant about his own abilities can also end up feeling badly about himself. Healthy self-esteem results when the right balance is attained. So the idea is to make a child feel capable. That doesn't mean the best or perfect, but capable of achieving his own goals.

No competition

One of the best ways to ensure that a child has good self-esteem is to avoid competition. Children learn at a very early age that others can do things better or before them, and if they are made to feel inadequate because they don't match up or cannot compete, irreparable damage can be done to their self-belief. We live in a competitive society, and many parents are more competitive about their children's achievements than ever – they want their children to read first, to walk first and shine amongst their peers.

It can be difficult for carers and teachers to make clear the message that all children develop at different stages, and that an early reader, for example, is not necessarily Mensa material. But it is a message that must be reiterated over and over again, and even passed on to children themselves. For example: 'Yes, it's wonderful that Sarah can read and count, but it's also wonderful that you build the best sandcastles in the sandpit'. Children need to be proud of their own genuine achievements, rather than being told that they are equal when they are clearly not.

The difference between self-respect and self-esteem

The over-emphasis on self-esteem in the past few years has caused parents to over-nurture, and to allow their children to get away with completely unacceptable behaviour in the belief that they have the right to express themselves and their unique characteristics. Children are praised for everything, even those things that are not praiseworthy. The result of this is, of course, that children become tyrants and they expect the world to bow to them.

Over-pampered children have no respect for anyone else and feel that they have a divine right to have their needs met. Not only is this a dangerous viewpoint, because children tend to believe that they are above or better than others and accepted rules, but they never actually develop self-respect. It is all too easy. Respect is earned. And a child who is not invested with self-respect will never fully understand the concept of discipline and accepted codes of behaviour, nor will he ever feel truly good about himself.

Now self-esteem is undoubtedly important. It involves having a positive self-image and feeling good about ourselves. We want that for the children in our care, but many parents and carers go in completely the opposite direction and give children a false sense of their own worth. They pump them up to the extent that they believe they are omnipotent, and from that point on they have their parents and carers over a barrel. They have learnt how to express themselves emotionally, they have accepted that they are the best, and they have very little time for anything other than praise and anything that increases their good feelings about themselves.

One of the problems with this is that the real world may not recognise a child's genius, and he will be set up for a nasty fall when he reaches adulthood, and even his late teens. The other problem is that discipline becomes more a question of 'softly, softly', rather than a realistic set of tools on which a child will rely as he makes decisions throughout his life.

The most important quality with which you can imbue a child is self-respect. It differs from self-esteem in several key ways. The first is that respect means a conscious understanding of strong points and limitations. It means children accepting themselves as they are, not as perfect children with expectations to live up to and an unreal sense of their own capabilities and weaknesses.

While esteem is awarded, respect must be earned through responsibility, co-operation and achievement. If we avoid the use of self-respect and substitute self-esteem, we have a convenient way of avoiding the effort required to succeed. For example, giving everyone a trophy simply because he participated in a race would increase everyone's self-esteem, but not their self-respect.

And to be honest, that self-esteem is based on hollow foundations, because any child will know in his heart that he didn't earn that trophy, and that it means less than something that is won as a result of real achievement and effort.

Why respect matters

When a child learns to respect himself, he also learns the ability to respect others – and other things, such as property, motivation, emotions, responsibility and authority. The reason is that he has earned his self-image and he can respect that. The process that led him there will be etched in his mind, and he will be able to draw upon that in different situations throughout his life, when dealing with others and when acting in society as a whole.

You cannot give a child self-respect, but you can ensure that he earns it by offering him opportunities to take responsibility, by giving him unqualified attention and unconditional love (hence enhancing his belief in himself as a unique individual, worthy of such attention). You can provide realistic goals and praise his attainment, rewarding genuine effort and achievement rather than blindly praising things that show no enterprise, initiative or effort. Encourage him to feel good about himself and his body by praising the things that make him special, by teaching respect for others, so that he can find the same things within himself.

It is clear that if we teach children the basics of respect, by imbuing them with self-respect from an early age, we can make them more selfless and more in tune with what others feel, think and need. The reason for this is that children who respect themselves have a clearer understanding of what it takes to succeed, to achieve, to meet their goals. Because they are respected themselves, they learn to respect others. Given the level of bullying, violence and crime in our society, this can only be a good thing.

Teaching self-respect

- Set realistic expectations and respect the efforts a child makes to attain them, whether they involve matters of discipline, school work, sports, interaction with other children, responsibility or just about anything else.
- Allow children the opportunity to succeed without the pressures of competition. Even small children are aware when other children appear to be better, faster or more advanced. You don't need to draw attention to this. Give them tasks at which they can succeed, and then reward genuine achievement and effort.
- Always reward and model respect. If you are respectful of children by listening to them, showing interest and seeing their point of view, they will learn to understand the concept and model the same behaviour. If we are rude to or dismissive of children – no matter how much we praise them – they will not learn respect for others, or develop self-respect. Praising every little thing about a child, while not taking the time to get to know them, to hear what they have to say and to make an attempt to understand their world, leaves them confused and does nothing to develop feelings of self-worth. Similarly, if they are praised for showing respect for others, they will learn that this is the type of behaviour that is expected and praised. And so it will continue.
- Don't overlook weaknesses. Children with a strong understanding of their own strengths and weaknesses are better equipped to deal with defeat, to understand others and to have a realistic view of their own capabilities. This doesn't mean highlighting them, but explaining that not everyone finds things easy, for example reading or turning a somersault. When a child is praised for things he knows in his heart he is not great at doing, he does not become more confident; he learns to distrust.

However, if he learns that a weakness is not necessarily a shortcoming, but a point from which to work, he will feel a lot more comfortable when tackling difficult activities in the future.

- Teach children that anything is possible, even if they do not believe they are capable. By setting challenges where they can succeed, they learn that shortcomings can be overcome, and that the idea is not to be the best, but to master the things that matter to them. Through that they develop a feeling of capability – and, as we saw earlier, this is the linchpin of genuine self-esteem.
- Praise the things that are unique to a child – personality, sense of humour, smile – anything that is special about him. He will learn to appreciate his own self-worth and feel good in his skin. And this teaches confidence. A confident child is much more likely to go ahead and succeed at the things he enjoys, and to respect his achievements.
- Do not go overboard or be false; children see straight through false praise. Instead, recognise effort, achievement, good qualities and a child's ideas. Show interest and pride. Show interest in him and his world. Be thrilled for his achievements, even if they do not live up to your expectations. If a child falls way behind in his reading programme, but shows a genuine willingness to learn, then make a fuss. If everything goes awry with early learning, but he's a great kid with spirit, manners and lots of friends, do not hesitate to focus on the aspects of his personality and approach to life that got him there. Praise everything genuinely good about a child and what he does. If he feels good about himself, if he believes you like him, flaws and all, he will develop self-esteem and self-respect that will spill over into every part of his life.
- Do not reward achievement that is not earned. It is simply not fair to reward all children regardless of effort or achievement. For one thing, it diminishes the achievement of those who have genuinely earned it – making children feel disgruntled and dispirited. Why bother, if everyone wins? For another thing, it does not give children any real impetus to try – to set and achieve goals. And that is where self-respect comes from.
- Offer plenty of opportunities for responsibility. A job well done, by a child himself, is hugely rewarding in itself. Children reap the rewards of their own effort. Responsibilities for small children can be as simple as having jobs in the nursery or at home, for which they are regularly responsible, such as feeding the fish, tidying up, emptying the bins or matching socks. Praise their efforts, even if they do not live up to expectations, and make sure those expectations are realistic in the first place.
- Take the time to explain why things matter – why jumping on someone's sofa might be offensive, why rattling sweet wrappers in the cinema is disruptive, why hitting someone makes them feel bad about themselves, how the destruction of someone else's property is insulting and hurtful. Put it in their terms, and help them to feel empathy and understanding for those around them in all kinds of different situations. If you teach your children respect for others, they will learn to understand the concept and develop a healthy respect for themselves. It is that simple.
- Avoid labels. Every time we use negative words to define children, they take them on board and file them away for future reference. No child will remember a particular incident, or be traumatised for life by being called stupid or slow or naughty, but these occasions form faulty bricks in the foundation of his self-image. No matter how much

you try to make up for it afterwards, if you have said something, your child believes it, even if it is on an unconscious level. And labels have a nasty way of becoming self-fulfilling prophecies. A child who grows up thinking he's not as good as his peers in some way, is seen as naughty or a slow reader, can end up building a negative picture of himself, which means that his self-esteem is not only low, but he has little or no respect for himself, nor confidence in himself.

A child who is praised without genuine grounds will never have a genuine sense of self-esteem, but an inflated sense of his own worth. In later life, such children have difficulty coming to terms with the idea that they do have some shortcomings and that they are not perfect. They also fail to realise that achievement requires effort, and that rewards are not handed out willy-nilly. Children with self-respect, however, are those who are given genuine praise for real achievement and effort, who learn to understand their weaknesses and strengths and use them to their best ability. They are more comfortable in their own skins, and more confident about themselves. Most importantly, however, they learn self-respect – because they've actually earned it, rather than having things handed to them on a plate. And children with self-respect have a much clearer understanding of others and are able to exhibit respect themselves.

Key points

- Self-esteem may get children further in the early days, but it does not instil a real sense of confidence or self-belief.
- Self-respect is a much better aim. Children with self-respect have a realistic view of themselves, and a self-belief based on genuine achievement and effort.
- Children with self-respect learn the concept of 'respect' and are able, therefore, to respect others, their property, authority figures, discipline and, maybe most importantly, themselves.
- Focus on both teaching and giving responsibility, setting reasonable expectations and challenges that can be mastered, and then reward genuine effort, initiative and achievement.

Chapter 22

Sharing

What is sharing?

Sharing is agreeably giving one's possessions to others. However, when a child is forced to give up his possession, it is not true sharing but rather surrender of property.

Teaching children to share is not an easy task, no matter how mild-mannered the child. But then, why should children share? Do we teach them in order to satisfy ourselves that the children in our care are loving and kind? Do we expect behaviour that even adults don't comply with? What should we be teaching children, and when?

Like most adults, children are naturally acquisitive. In other words, they see something and they covet it, no matter who has it or how much it costs. Similarly, things that belong to or are being played with by other children have an irresistibility which the average child will have difficulty suppressing. Again, that's not too different from adults, who often have a head firmly turned in the direction of the Jones' or the latest gadgets. These instincts and desires are natural and even healthy – they have fired up ambition and motivated people to better themselves for centuries. So teaching sharing is going against a child's natural instinct, and no matter what the age of your pre-schooler, it is going to be difficult.

But let's look at it this way. You are at university and you are using the only computer in the building to finish an assignment. Someone comes along and demands to use it. Do you instantly relinquish the computer because you need to share? Does anyone come along and tell you that you have to give it up because someone else wants it, or you've had your turn? Unlikely. Chances are you will explain that you are using the computer and agree a time that you will be finished. Most people will respect your right to continue with something you had first.

Change the situation to a pre-school classroom. Child A is playing with the toy trains. Child B comes along and asks for them. Child A resists. Does the teacher then step in and say that Child A has to give them up? Why? The fact is that Child A had them first, and has every right to continue with a game in which he is engrossed. Asking the child to relinquish the toys does several things:

- Teaches the child that nothing really belongs to him, and that others have the right to take what is theirs simply because they are there. Forcing a child to give up a possession for no other reason than someone else wants it will only make them want to protect their possessions even more energetically in the future.
- It backs a child into a corner and makes him powerless, which is a big cue for tantrums, anger and frustration.

- It teaches him that he has no rights – while giving Child B rights that he did not actually earn. Child A got there first, and Child B needs to learn to wait. It is one of life's realities. Nothing usually happens just because you want it to, and it is a lesson that all children need to learn.
- It teaches the child not to take pride in his possessions. If he can be usurped at a moment's notice, why should he take care of them or develop a keen interest?
- It teaches a child that adults will intervene to give him what he wants – which means that he will never learn to negotiate or even share of his own accord.

So what is the right way to deal with sharing? Obviously we cannot raise a generation of completely selfish children who never learn to give or share. The simple answer is this: offer choices and teach negotiation. Child B has a choice. He can ask Child A to share as soon as he has finished or he can ask to play alongside. Another option is to find something else to do until Child A has finished. Child A also has a choice. He can decide when he has finished, and share the toys. Or he can allow Child B to play with them.

What do the children learn? Problem-solving, and, of course, authority and control. Most importantly, children learn to wait and they learn to solve problems without the intervention of an adult. Most children are keener to share when they are not forced to do so. In fact, when in control, most children are positively magnanimous.

Won't share, no matter what!

Some children dig in their heels and refuse to share, despite all efforts to encourage negotiation. They may hang on to a particular toy or material every day and refuse ever to give it up. Consider the motivation: some children have an overwhelming need to have their own personal possessions. Maybe they come from large families where nothing is their own. Or maybe they have few possessions due to impoverishment, and they relish the chance to own an object, even part-time.

If this is the case, it is important to develop a fair system. In other words, if there are two children who want to use the same toy, and there is an hour of playtime, a timer can be set at 30 minutes to provide equitable use. A ride around the playground, or 30 swings on the set, can mean the end of the use of a toy. Putting a system like this into play at the outset means that no child feels singled out. These are the rules, and they are fair to everyone.

A child who has never had to share may also find it difficult to understand the concept. Ensuring that your child (or any child in your care) is regularly in contact with other children in a social setting will help to encourage the idea.

Playing board games can help – children learn that there are rules, that they need to wait their turn, and that everyone can be involved in a game. They also need to learn to ask other children politely in order to get permission to do things. These are skills that will continue to develop into adulthood. Make sure, too, that there are always other options. There is no point in creating a problem where there doesn't need to be one. If there are lots of toys and activities to choose from, a spat is much less likely. Another good idea is to read stories about sharing– and the good feelings that it can imbue. Planting a seed in a possessive child's mind can do no harm. Good books to try include *Mine* by Miriam Cohen, *Mine, Mine, Mine! A Little Help With Sharing* by Sheryl Berk and Josie Yess, *Share Said the Rooster* by Pamela Allen and *Why Should I Share?* by Clare Llewellyn and Mike Gordon.

Mine!

It is not unusual for young children to see everything as their own. When they first begin to play, children play alongside other children rather than with them, which means that they do not immediately learn that toys can be shared. Pre-schoolers often tend to have an overt interest in what belongs to whom, and a passionate desire to claim everything as their own. 'Mine!' is often one of the first words in a toddler's vocabulary. There is nothing wrong with ownership. Children have a right to own things, and to learn to take care of them. But at the same time, it is important to understand and respect others and their needs.

Dr Christopher Greene, author of *Toddler Taming*, has a tried and tested series of golden rules which he uses in his own household. They can be applied to a nursery, early childhood education centre, or in your own home. He suggests the following:

- If you want to use something that belongs to someone else, you must ask first. When the children go to visit someone else, we are teaching them not to run and grab the toys, but to ask (unless, of course, the toy is offered). When others come over, our children can relax knowing that we will gently defend their possessions – 'In our home, we ask each other before playing with others people's things.'
- When someone asks to use your things, you can't simply say: 'No'. Nor do you have to say yes. But if you decline to share, respect the other enough to either give a reason or suggest an alternative, such as: 'Let's take turns', or 'You can play with it, but only inside', or 'That is my very favourite, but you can play with any of these.'
- Remember the golden rule: 'Do to others as you would have done to you'. This comes in handy when considering how to answer someone who wants to play with your things. It helps you decide, too, when and what to ask of someone else ('I know he just got that new toy, and I like to play with my new toys'). This rule is also a wonderful guide for how to handle and care for other people's things when you are using them.

Try not to be concerned if it takes some time for a child to learn the concept of sharing. For some people it can actually take a lifetime to become less proprietorial. Remember that taking a great interest in one activity or item is a healthy part of development, and it can foster creativity, pride in possessions, long-term interests and, ultimately, the art of negotiation. Sharing should not be about teaching children that other people's rights are more important than their own, but that others share interests and have rights alongside their own. Demanding that a child share does not truly teach him to share, but teaches resentment and the idea that sharing is painful. The greatest irony is that given choices, most children will be delighted to share. A little feeling of power can go a long way.

Key points

- Addressing the issue of sharing is important before implementing a policy. Ask yourself what the meaning of sharing is before forcing a child to do so.
- Create time slots for popular toys at the outset, so that no child feels singled out to share.
- Teaching negotiation, respect and the importance of waiting are more important than teaching children that they have a divine right to an activity or a toy.
- Giving a child choices and empowering him will make him more likely to share of his own accord, which is the true heart of sharing.

Chapter 23

Shyness

In most shy children, bashfulness and timidity represent a personality trait rather than a fault, and some children are simply more temperamentally shy than others. Parents, carers and teachers can often fail to see the good points of a shy child, and feel that he is simply socially inadequate when there is really no problem. However, shyness can sometimes indicate a manifestation of inner problems, not inner peace, and it's important to keep an eye on children who withdraw, particularly if they do so suddenly.

According to child development experts and researchers, problematic shyness involves anxiety and inhibited behaviour in social situations. It occurs most frequently in situations that are new or those in which a child believes he is standing out or being evaluated. Although all children may experience shyness sometimes, some children experience shyness to a debilitating degree.

According to a 1993 study, young shy children often show an apparent eagerness to observe others, but combine this with a reluctance to speak to or join the others. For example, shy children may remain silent around unfamiliar others, even when spoken to. They may refuse to enter a new setting such as a classroom without being accompanied by a parent. Shy children may refuse to participate in athletic or dance activities, they may look at the ground when with unfamiliar individuals and they may go to great lengths to avoid calling attention to themselves.

Most shy children want to interact with unfamiliar others, but don't because of their fear. A different problem exists when a child simply prefers to be alone. These loner children, who are rare, show little or no interest in observing others and little or no excitement when approached by others. This type of problem must be addressed by a mental health professional.

What makes a child shy?

Shyness experts identify four main possible causes:

- genes predisposing a person to shyness
- a less than firm attachment bond between parent and child
- poor acquisition of social skills
- parents, siblings or others harshly and frequently teasing or criticising a child.

The good news is that there are many ways to encourage a shy child to develop socially, to feel comfortable with himself and confident enough to interact with others. It's worth noting that a shy child is unlikely to become the class clown, but there are lovely elements to shyness and it's worth remembering these.

Chapter 23: Shyness

Not all bad news

Research undertaken in 1996 has found that shy children tend to engage in significantly less social misbehaviour than other children. This may occur because shy children care so much about what others think of them. Shyness can be a help or a handicap to a child, depending partly on how it's handled. Shy children tend to be attentive listeners, and can be very peaceful to be with. Outgoing children can, over time, become exhausting, even if they exude brightness and extrovert tendencies; a shy child can be a delight – a comfortable presence.

Many people don't understand shyness and equate being shy with having a problem. They believe a shy child must suffer from poor self-image. Most of the time this label couldn't be more unfair. Many shy children have a solid self-concept. They have an inner peace that shines. A shy child with healthy self-worth makes eye-to-eye contact, is polite and seems happy with himself. He is just quiet. His behaviour is generally good; he is a nice child to be with, and people are comfortable in his presence.

The worrying side

The practical and emotional problems caused by shyness are apparent. As a practical matter, shy children obtain less practice of social skills and develop fewer friends. They tend to avoid activities, such as sports, drama and debate, which would put them in the limelight. According to 1986 research, shy children also tend to be perceived as unfriendly and untalented, and they can feel lonely and have low self-esteem. Recent research indicates that shy children can become anxious teens, but this is not obviously always the case.

When a child is more than naturally shy, he withdraws. He avoids eye-to-eye contact and has a lot of behavioural problems. People are not comfortable in his presence. When you delve into this little person, you discover he operates from anger and fear instead of peace and trust. When you delve deeper, you often find he has a lot to be angry about. Problems at home? Jealousy? Stress? There are many causes, and they may simmer away beneath the quiet surface.

Some children also hide behind a shy label so that they don't have to reveal a self they don't like. It's safer not to show anything, so they retreat into a protective shell. The shy label becomes an excuse for not developing social skills and a reason for not exercising them. An unmotivated child can use the shy label as a defence against trying harder and an excuse for staying at the same level of skill development. For these children, shyness is a handicap, reinforcing their weak self-esteem. To cure the shyness, you must build up the self-esteem. These children need parents, carers and teachers they can trust, who discipline in a way that does not lead to internalised anger and self-dislike.

How you can help

- Don't assume that shyness is a problem. A shy child can be sensitive, deeply caring and reserved – slow to warm up to strangers, approaches social relationships cautiously, but generally seems to be a happy person.

- It's tempting to want to help a shy child become more outgoing. But be careful – the more you pull, the more some children recoil. You can't pull a child out of shyness. It's better to create a comfortable environment that lets his social personality develop naturally.
- Never label a child 'shy', which makes even a young child feel that something's wrong with him. It will make him feel shyer. Choose more positive terms if you must use a label, such as 'quiet', 'private' or 'reserved'.
- Introduce a child to new situations gradually. Talk about what is coming beforehand and then allow him to proceed at his own pace. You cannot make a shy child outgoing by instructing him, but you can teach him to be polite, and to learn what is expected of him in various situations. Saying hello and making eye-to-eye contact should really be enough. Do not expect more.
- Keep the attention off the child in difficult or new situations until he becomes comfortable.
- In new situations, encourage a shy child to bring along a favourite activity, which can be used as a bridge to communication.
- Don't put a shy child on the spot and expect him to perform. You may want him to sing his new nursery song for his grandparents, but if you spring your request on him, he'll undoubtedly run. Give fair warning, and privately ask a child's permission first. This shows respect.
- Don't interrupt or speak for a shy child. This will only compound the problem and undermine potentially fragile self-esteem. Be reserved yourself and a shy child will become more outgoing.
- Tell the child about times when you felt shy. Once shy children start to feel negative about being shy, they may enter a downward spiral of becoming less and less confident and having lower and lower self-esteem. Help to counter this by disclosing the times when you acted shy yourself. Children often view adults as powerful, godlike figures, so this will help children to feel better about their own shy behaviour.
- While you do not want children to assume that being shy is a negative quality, it may be necessary for them to overcome some elements of their shyness in order to develop socially and to be able to interact well with others. One of the best ways to bring this about is to explain the value of becoming more outgoing – in order to do something, such as buy sweets at the sweetshop. 'I had to learn to overcome my shyness and talk to the shopkeeper', for example. Or explain the more immediate value to the child of outgoing behaviour, such as making more friends, having more fun and enjoying school or nursery and other social activities more.
- Show empathy when the child is afraid to interact. By showing empathy, you can ensure the child feels understood and accepted, which also helps the child identify and talk about his emotions and start searching for a way to control them.
- Avoid labels. Children who are told that they are shy tend to start thinking of themselves as shy and then fulfil the role, without making any effort to change.
- Set goals for more outgoing behaviour and measure progress. A good deal of research supports the value of goal-setting in improving performance of various types, even in small children. The most useful goals are those that are measurable (quantifiable), challenging yet realistic, and are set with the involvement of the person whose

performance (behaviour) is in question. For many shy children a realistic, challenging goal is to say at least one word to one new person every day. Other possibly appropriate goals might include speaking in front of a whole nursery class, joining (even silently) in play with another child or asking an adult a question. Parents can help children see their progress by posting a chart at home that shows a star for each day the child achieved the goal.

- Be a role model. Children learn a great deal through observing the behaviour of parents and others. Parents who never invite anyone over to the house, who never take phone calls and who never speak to strangers may tend to have shy or non-social children. Parents who want their children to act in a more outgoing way are wise to monitor their own behaviour and appear outgoing whenever possible in front of the children. Invite friends and family members over, visit neighbours and speak to pleasant looking strangers at the supermarket. Most importantly, talk with children the age of your child – join them in their games. If your child won't speak or join in, don't worry – you're setting a model that shows that acting outgoing is something you do with children and that the children usually respond well.
- Give a child experience of unfamiliar people and situations. The more practice shy children get interacting with unfamiliar people the faster the shyness will decrease. However, the exposure will work best if it is gradual. Whenever possible, let the child get used to the setting and people before you push the child to interact. Help the child develop confidence in one new setting at a time, little by little.
- Prompt shy children to speak, join or interact with others whenever there is any chance that they will do so. Specific prompts work best. If the child won't say anything to a person, try prompting him to wave hello or goodbye. Be careful not to push a shy child too hard. You could just create more resistance. Go for gradual improvement, realising that the child will show improvement some days and not others.
- Praise others' outgoing behaviour in the presence of a shy child. By positively commenting on the outgoing behaviour of others, you can help a shy child come to value outgoing behaviour while learning the specifics of the behaviour.
- Help him practise interacting with others. Some shy children do not know what to say in certain situations, such as when they meet a new child. You can help shy children by encouraging them to practise social skills.
- Shy children can benefit from reading books about children who overcome shyness or fears. Good ones to try include *Shy Sophie* (by Tony Garth), *Little Miss Shy* (by Roger Hargreaves) and *I'm Shy* (by Karen Bryant-Mole).
- Social rejection and teasing can help produce shy behaviour. So do not tease a shy child or allow anyone else to. If necessary, remove him from the presence of rejecting or teasing.
- Shy children can best start to control their feelings of embarrassment and fear when the children identify and talk about the feelings. To help the children develop these skills, talk about your emotions in front of them. For instance, say 'I feel frightened when you climb up there'.
- One of the best ways to bring a shy child out of his shell is to associate him with a child who is very outgoing and outspoken. Often, just being around this other child will change both children's behaviours, each taking cues from the other and letting their personalities

wear off in the process. The outspoken child may calm down a bit and your shy one will be a bit louder. Another way is to introduce your child to another child who is even more withdrawn or shy than he is, if that is possible. This will often give the child a sense of power and nurturing as he tries to help the other child feel more comfortable. After all, your child knows how the other child feels and will feel empathy and want to help.
- Encourage your child to be a part of your conversations and try to make him feel like a valuable part of the family or classroom with an important opinion. These things may help you see the more outgoing side of your child eventually and gain some friends in the process.

Shy children can be a joy to be around, even if they are a source of discomfiture to some parents and carers. When the more quietly confident and sensitive elements of their nature are celebrated, shy children can become happy, healthy adults with perfectly normal social skills. But beware of the negative elements of shyness, and don't allow a child to hide behind a mask or a label – chronically shy children might need prompting to be polite and more outgoing in order to make friends and develop normally. The good news is that even the most bashful child can, with gentle prompting, avoid the problems associated with shyness and be comfortable and happy in any situation.

Key points

- Don't immediately leap to the conclusion that shyness is a problem. Some of the nicest children are shy and will continue to be.
- Sometimes shyness can mask a problem, such as poor self-esteem, stress or anger or even poor parental bonding. If a child does not seem happy, content and confident, it's worth considering potential causes for his shyness.
- If a child needs bringing out of his shell in order to make friends and develop, avoid labelling him and work on positive strategies to make him more outgoing in social situations.

Chapter 24

Sibling Rivalry

Sibling rivalry is jealousy, competition and fighting between brothers and sisters. It is a concern for almost all parents of two or more children and can also be an issue for carers who look after more than one member of the family at a time. Sibling rivalry usually continues throughout childhood and can be very frustrating and stressful for parents and carers. There are many things you can do to help children get along better and work through conflicts in positive ways.

Most siblings' relationships will eventually develop into something close, and working through problems provides children with a chance to develop important skills, such as co-operating and being able to see another point of view. However, unlike the ties between parents and children, the connection among siblings is a horizontal one. That is, siblings exist on the same plane – as peers, more or less equals. This provides plenty of scope for rivalry.

Although one may be stronger or more dominant than others, brothers and sisters rarely exert the kind of power and authority over one another that parents hold over their children. Nor are there rules, codes of behaviour for different stages of life or biblical commandments mandating siblings to respect and honour one another as they must respect and honour parents. As a result, they are freer, more open and generally more honest with one another than they are with parents, and less fearful of punishment or rejection.

As children, they say what is on their minds, without censoring their words or concerning themselves about the long-term effects of their emotions on one another. Even as adults, many siblings speak more bluntly to each other than they dare to friends or colleagues. They also develop an innate ability to find and use just the right buttons to wind up siblings – something that is even carried into adulthood. They find a weakness, a point of insecurity, and hit hard.

Treating children differently

It is perfectly normal, natural and appropriate for parents and carers to have different feelings towards each of the children in their care, and to treat those children differently. The challenge they always face is to appreciate what is unique about each child, and to show that appreciation in a balanced way so that over the course of years, all children feel equally loved and valued. Parents and carers fail in that challenge when the line between different treatment and preferential treatment becomes muddied and, without ever realising it, they begin to slip from one to the other.

Unintentionally, on their part, the most achieving child, the most affectionate one, the first born or the last, the one most like or unlike a parent or relative can move from a position of equality with other children to one of receiving or seeming to receive special attention. Parents and carers may not be aware of slipping from a normal course of treating children differently to giving one preferential treatment, but siblings – whether children, adolescents or adults – are highly sensitive to such slips. And the more so because they pick up signals of favouritism not only from the way parents and carers behave towards them but also from behaviour towards their brothers and sisters.

Young children monitor their parents' and carers' treatment of their siblings, just as they monitor their own treatment, and that relationship of parent or carer to siblings becomes as important as the relationship of parent to self. It is certainly true that what young children label as favouritism may be far from the real thing.

Perceiving inequality

But herein lies the crux of the problem. It's perception rather than reality that colours a sibling relationship. If a child perceives that he is being treated less fairly, even if parents are scrupulously fair, he will feel disempowered and more likely to initiate rivalry.

Sibling rivalry is exhausting for everyone involved, and often siblings are the only outlet that stressed children have to exert control, to lash out, to scrap, fight, bicker, taunt, tease and harass. You will often see children exhibiting horrendous behaviour with siblings, and it can be a sign that things are just too much.

Although advice books admonish parents and carers not to compare their children, but to view each only as an individual, most find it almost impossible not to make some comparisons. It is when the comparisons turn into labels used to define and pigeonhole children that they may become problematic. Labels stuck on in early childhood become part of the internal image children have of themselves, later to be incorporated into the roles they assume with each other and in the world outside the family.

The obvious causes of sibling rivalry

- Each child is competing to define who he is as an individual. As he discovers who he is, he tries to find his own talents, activities and interests. He wants to show that he is separate from his siblings.
- Children feel they are getting unequal amounts of attention, discipline and responsiveness.
- Children may feel their relationship with their parents is threatened by the arrival of a new baby.
- A child's developmental stages affect how well he can share attention and get along with a sibling.
- Children who are hungry, bored or tired are more likely to start arguments.
- Children may not know positive ways to get attention from their brother or sister, so they start arguments as a means of doing so.
- Family dynamics play a role. For example, one child may remind a parent of a relative who was particularly difficult, and this may subconsciously influence how the parent treats that child.

- Children will fight more with each other in families where there is no understanding that fighting is not an acceptable way to resolve conflicts.
- Families who don't share enjoyable times together will probably have more conflict.
- Stress in the parents' lives can decrease the amount of attention given to the children and increase sibling rivalry.
- Stress in a child's life can shorten fuses, and create more conflict.

What can you do?

- Never compare children. Comparison is the single biggest cause of sibling rivalry, and it must be avoided at all cost, no matter how tempting.
- Don't typecast. Let each child be who he is. Don't try to pigeonhole or label children.
- Don't play favourites. Most children go through easy and difficult patches, and although it's common to side with or feel more affectionate towards the good one, it will do you no favours in the long run. In the end, difficult children are often those most in need of attention and care.
- Set your household or classroom around co-operation rather than competition. For example, have them race the clock to pick up toys, instead of racing each other.
- Pay attention to the time of day and other patterns in when conflicts usually occur. Perhaps a change in the routine, an earlier meal or snack, or a well-planned activity when the children are at loose ends could help avert conflicts.
- Teach children positive ways to get attention from each other. Show them how to approach another child and ask them to play.
- Being fair is very important, but it is not the same as being equal. Children need to learn that you will do your best to meet each of their unique needs. Even if you are able to do everything totally equally, children will still feel as if they're not getting a fair share of attention, discipline or responsiveness from you.
- Plan activities that are fun for everyone. If children have good experiences together, it acts as a buffer when they come into conflict. It's easier to work it out with someone with whom you share warm memories.
- Make sure each child has enough time and space of their own. Children need chances to do their own thing, play with their own friends without their sibling and they need to have their space and property protected.
- Set aside 'alone' time for each child. Each parent or carer should spend some one-on-one time with each child on a regular basis. Try to get in at least a few minutes each day. It's amazing how much even just ten minutes of uninterrupted one-on-one time can mean to a child.
- When you are alone with each child, ask them once in a while what they like most and least about each brother and sister. This will help you keep tabs on their relationships, and also remind you that they probably do have some positive feelings for each other.
- Celebrate children's differences.
- Let each child know he is special—just for who he is.

Resolving conflicts

- Research shows that while you should pay attention to children's conflicts (so that no one gets hurt, and you notice abuse if it occurs), it's best not to intervene. When parents and carers jump into sibling spats, they often protect one child (usually the younger sibling) against the other (usually the older one). This escalates the conflict, because the older child resents the younger, and the younger feels that they can get away with more since the adult appears to be on their side.
- Help children to develop the skills to work out their conflicts on their own. Teach them how to compromise, respect one another and divide things fairly. Give them the tools, then express your confidence that they can work it out by saying: 'I'm sure you can work out a solution.' Don't get drawn in.
- It doesn't matter who started it, because it takes two to argue. Hold children equally responsible when ground rules get broken.
- In a conflict, give children a chance to express their feelings about each other. Don't try to talk them out of their feelings. Help them to find words for their feelings. Show them how to talk about their feelings, without yelling, name-calling or violence.
- Encourage win-win negotiations, where each side gains something.
- Provide children with reminders. When they start picking on each other, help them remember how to state their feelings to each other. Don't solve the problem for them, just help them remember how to problem solve.
- Teach conflict resolution skills during calm times. In other words, suggest ways of negotiating a compromise (you have a turn and then I will), teaching children to say 'No, I don't like that' when they are unhappy rather than lashing out, and seeking the help of an adult if they find that a situation is difficult to manage.
- Model good conflict resolution skills.
- Dangerous fights need to be stopped immediately. Separate the children. When they have calmed down, talk about what happened and make it very clear that no violence is ever allowed.
- Involve children in setting ground rules. Ground rules, with clear and consistent consequences for breaking them, can help prevent many squabbles.
- Give each child responsibility. Resist the trap of giving an oldest child all the household chores. There is no reason why he has to do everything, just because of his age. His younger siblings can also help, for example, by tidying toys. And an oldest child does not need to take his younger siblings with him whenever he goes out to play.

Sensitive parenting can restore the balance and, in many cases, often prevent serious rivalry from taking hold. Remember to make each of child feel special. Older or younger, every child needs to feel that she is as important as anyone else in the family. If one child thinks that her sibling is held in higher esteem, then jealousy will arise. Do your best to listen to each child and respond to him positively. Above all, respect all the children in your care. Every child has the same psychological need to be loved and accepted, no matter what position he has in the family. He has feelings and ideas that he wants to express, and he has a right to receive respect, and to be taken seriously, whether he is the youngest, middle or oldest child.

Chapter 24: Sibling Rivalry

Remember that children will lash out at each other from time to time, and it's completely normal. Try to teach them other ways of relieving frustration and anger, and make it clear that it is not acceptable to treat others in ways that they would not like to be treated themselves. Above all, show some understanding and patience. Sibling rivalry occurs in almost every family at some point or another, and you need to look at places where the balance of power or attention may have shifted, or when one or more of your children need some extra love and time.

Key points

- Sibling rivalry is completely natural and occurs in almost all families.
- There are many causes, but a shift in the balance of power or attention is almost always at the root.
- Young children often fight and argue as a way of getting the other's attention; teaching them better methods of communication as well as co-operation can help.
- Celebrate differences, avoid competition and show enthusiasm for every child's achievements.
- When rivalry declines into regular bickering, it's usually best to ignore it. Children need to learn to sort out their problems, negotiate and find a happy middle ground. If you constantly intervene, they will always expect you to.
- Make kindness to siblings a household policy and reward all efforts towards this goal. Children will soon see that it's easier to get along than it is to waste energy fighting a useless cause.

Chapter 25

Stress

The problem of stress in young children has recently been the subject of intensive research, and it is now clear that even pre-schoolers are vulnerable to both its physical and emotional effects. In many cases, behaviour which appears to be disruptive, regressive or even simply attention-seeking may well be a manifestation of stress, and it is something that teachers and carers must address in order to ensure the welfare and learning potential of children.

Traditionally, stress has been defined in terms of its cause – in other words, whether it is internal or external. Internal sources of stress include hunger, pain, sensitivity to noise, temperature change and crowding, fatigue and over- or under-stimulation in a child's immediate physical environment. External stressors can include separation from family, change in family composition, exposure to arguing and interpersonal conflict, exposure to violence, experiencing the aggression of others (bullying), loss of important personal property or a pet, exposure to excessive expectations for accomplishment, hurrying and disorganisation in a child's daily life events.

Although many studies appear to focus on single stressors, in real life children experience stress from all sorts of directions. A study carried out in 2000 found that multiple stressors interact with one another, and can have a cumulative effect.

How well do children cope with stress?

All people, including children, have a stress threshold, which is basically a point after which they cannot cope or adapt. This threshold is unique to individuals, and is based on a child's developmental level, previous life experience, their coping skill inventory and, indeed, their physiology.

Researchers suggest that children under the age of six are developmentally less capable of:

(1) thinking about an event in its entirety;
(2) Selecting from a menu of possible behaviours in response to any new, interesting, or anxiety-inducing event;
(3) comprehending an event separate from their own feelings;
(4) modifying their physical reactions in response to a change in stimuli.

The younger the child, the greater the impact of new events, and the more powerful and potentially negative stress becomes. Some stress is a normal part of a child's everyday life and can have positive influences. However, excessive stress can have both immediate and far-reaching effects on children's adaptability to new situations, even events that are seemingly unrelated to the specific stressful event.

Chapter 25: Stress

How do children experience stress?

In 1982, the researcher L. Zegans theorised that stress is experienced in four somewhat distinct stages:

(1) alarm and physical reaction;
(2) appraisal, as a child attempts to make meaning from the event;
(3) searching for adaptation and coping strategies; and finally
(4) implementation of a strategy or strategies.

This implementation stage may be a one-time action or may be extended over hours or days. Children's appraisal of stressful events and their choices of viable coping strategies are different from those used by adults. In addition, experts have observed that children's physical responses to stress are also different from adult responses in that they may be more intense and involve the whole body.

How does stress manifest itself in children?

Change is a natural part of the development of children. However, no two children experience change in exactly the same way. Children may benefit from different types of support. Look for both positive and negative behaviours that are not the norm for the child. Noticeable emotional, social, physical and intellectual changes may be a signal to check out the possibility of stress as a factor:

- Emotionally, a child under stress may appear more fearful, sensitive, tense, aggressive, greedy, angry, restless or irritable. If the child does not know why he feels this way, stress could be a factor.
- Socially, a child under stress may be more aggressive or withdrawn. Both of these symptoms can lead to feelings of isolation, which may increase stress levels.
- Physically, children under stress may be more prone to accidents, illness, ulcers or headaches. They may have lower energy levels or trouble with constipation or diarrhoea, even though they are apparently healthy. They may bite their fingernails. Regressive behaviour is also very common.
- Intellectually, children under stress may be easily distracted or restless. They may have difficulty concentrating or making decisions. Their expression may seem dull or vacant. They may be preoccupied with images of monsters or other threats or daydream more than usual.

Experts also suggest that children's reactions to stress may manifest themselves in depression and avoidance, excessive shyness, hyper-vigilance, excessive worrying, freezing up in social situations, appearing to have obsessive interest in objects, routines, food, persistent concern about what comes next and excessive clinging.

Does it cause real problems?

Stress interferes with the short-term memory, which is electrical in form and very easily disrupted. It is housed in the limbic system and is the brain's clearing house or control centre. All information flows in and out of the limbic system. Stress interrupts the flow of information in and out of the centre, so learning and memory are disrupted. It affects all of us this way, but especially children and very often boys.

To combat problems within his life a child's subconscious will develop defences to keep the trauma of failure to a minimum – in other words, apparent laziness, withdrawal, selective deafness, defiance and school avoidance. The fear of failure in itself is a major obstacle to learning. It may sound silly to assume that pre-schoolers are worried about failure, but so many parents these days are hyper-anxious that their children are developing normally, that they are intellectually adequate, keeping up with their peers, and good at everything from ballet to identifying colours, that many children soon pick up on the fact that they are not somehow living up to expectations. The fear of letting down parents, teachers and carers can be a dramatic source of stress for children, and impact on their learning.

Adapting to stress

The behaviours which children adopt in an attempt to cope with stress are really just struggles to manage and react to stressful events. Children generally distance themselves emotionally from stressful situations by behaving in ways to diminish the stress (crying or being upset when a parent leaves them at school or nursery, for example) or acting in ways that conceal feelings of vulnerability (being aggressive or disruptive). As they become older, children learn to use problem-solving strategies to cope with stress by asking questions about events, circumstances and expectations of what will happen, and clarification of what has happened.

What does this mean for teachers and carers?

First of all, although you are unlikely to be the source of stress, events within your setting can add to a child's load, particularly if they are vulnerable or under pressure in other areas of their lives. If you notice a child's behaviour changing in any of the ways above, it is very likely that they are under pressure and it will help immeasurably if you can reduce potential stresses in your own environment in whatever way possible. A child who is constantly asking questions about routines, or what comes next, or what is required of him, is likely to be taking the first steps towards coping with things themselves, and although it can be intensely irritating, it is important that these questions are patiently answered.

What can you do?

Help children to anticipate stressful events, such as a change in routine, a change in classroom or teacher. Encourage parents to explain potentially stressful situations at home (such as a new baby, a move, or even a first haircut), so that you have an understanding of what might be causing problems. You can then work through the problems by increasing a child's understanding of an anticipated event.

- Provide supportive environments where children can play out or use art materials to express their concerns. Painting, drawing and dancing are good tools for stress relief, both emotionally and physically. Some children may adopt rather wild behaviour, given the chance, but look at it as an opportunity for them to let off steam.
- Use books as a point of discussion for fears and new situations, such as having a new baby, moving house, bullies, fear of the dark, and other common worries. Good choices include: *The Owl Who Was Afraid of the Dark* by Jill Tomlinson and Paul Howard, *Poems About Being Scared* by Brian Moses and Mike Gordon, *When I'm Feeling Scared* by Trace Moroney, *My New Baby*, by Annie Kubler and *Big Ernie's New Home* by Teresa Martin and Whitney Martin.
- Consider using a circle time to address difficult issues which children may be facing. Go around the circle and encourage each child to express a worry and ask the others to help come up with solutions. It may sound advanced for pre-schoolers, but you will be amazed at the strategies that children can develop on their own.
- Help children to work out their own coping strategies. For example, if a child feels unhappy with teasing (even mild teasing, which should not normally have an impact), encourage them to ask for help or to tell the other children that they do not like it. It may sound simplistic, but coping strategies help children to feel more effective in stressful situations.
- Work on emotional literacy. Encourage children to recognise, name, accept and then express their feelings appropriately.
- If a child seems extremely out of control and inconsolable, angry or frightened, teach him some very basic relaxation techniques. Help him to take three deep breaths, or to count from five backwards, or to dance, imagine a favourite place, or even tense and relax his muscles. What you do here is to provide him with an immediate way of releasing tension, and he will be calm enough then to consider coping strategies.
- Set realistic expectations for each child's developmental level.
- Take the time to develop mutual respect and trust between you and the children. A lot of this comes down to listening carefully when a child speaks to you, and showing respect for what they think and feel. Being dismissive simply undermines their trust in you.
- Model appropriate ways to deal with stress and change. If everything goes haywire in your classroom or home, try to show children how you deal with it, rather than panicking or losing your temper. And if you do lose it, apologise afterwards and explain how you were feeling.
- Allow time for children to share their thoughts. Plan time for children to play alone, and in small and large groups.
- Remember the value of laughter.
- Nurture and cherish all of the children in your care. Accept them for who they are.
- Guide each child by letting him know when behaviour is acceptable. Verbally recognise positive behaviour.

- Contribute to each child's positive self-esteem by providing encouragement.
- When unacceptable behaviour occurs, redirect children by stating their options. Help them find acceptable ways to express negative feelings.
- Other strategies include implementing sound positive discipline strategies, following consistent routines, enhancing co-operation and providing time for children to safely disclose their concerns and stresses privately and in groups.
- Do not be afraid to discuss your concerns with a child's parents. It may be that their child is acting beautifully at home in an attempt not to cause further problems, and they may not be aware that the child needs extra help, love and attention and, in the extreme, some professional help to deal with stress and pressure.

Children are not emotionally mature enough to deal with stress, and small things in a child's life can disrupt his equilibrium, inhibit social development and learning and have physical and emotional effects. It is not normally one thing that tips the balance, and it is important to see any change in a child's behaviour as a potential manifestation of stress. You may not be aware of the cause (or, indeed, multiple causes) and it may even be frustrating to deal with a child who flies off the handle, bursts into tears or clings at the slightest provocation. But young children do not have the coping strategies or rationalisation that adults do, and they require guidance, support, patience, understanding and productive skills in order to deal with what they perceive to be difficult situations.

Key points

- We are only just beginning to understand the impact of stress in children. One in ten children in the UK now suffers from a serious mental disorder, and children as young as three are being treated for stress-related and emotional problems. Research by Young Minds, the mental health charity, shows a huge increase in recent years in the number of children, as young as four, seeking treatment for severe mental health problems.
- It is likely to be a series of stressors or problems causing a stress reaction, rather than one single issue, although it may be one that tips a child over.
- It helps practitioners if they become familiar with the physical and emotional manifestations of stress. They are then more able to help the children.
- Offer patient support, regular routines and plenty of explanations throughout your day, to help children know where they stand.
- Encourage children to develop coping and problem-solving skills through discussion, artwork and even individual interaction.
- Remember that stress can affect both a child's ability to learn and to sleep well, which can further impact learning. A slow child may feel worse if he feels he is not living up to expectations. Ensure that you set reasonable expectations and applaud all effort, regardless of achievement.
- Mention your concerns to parents, who may not be aware of the problem.

Chapter 26

Swearing

Everyone has a different tolerance threshold for swearing and, with the frequent use of profanities in our popular culture, many of us have become largely immune to words which would once have shocked. However, there is surely nothing as disturbing or offensive as hearing a young child swear. And swear they do – teachers and carers in all sectors report hearing swearing on a regular basis. Not only has it become a way of gaining status and street cred among children, but many swear words have now been adopted into the English language and have become commonplace expressions of emotion. Whatever the reasons for the increase – and there are many – young children need to learn to express themselves appropriately and to learn that swearing is, in many cases, verbal abuse and always highly offensive. Let's look at why young children swear and what you can do to turn things around.

Normal behaviour

There is no doubt that experimentation with dirty words is a normal part of development. Children repeat powerful or offensive words which they hear adults use; they may even make up unique words to use as insults. Several studies show that most normal children enjoy using language in jokes, puns and stories that adults find disgusting. Young children will freely use scatological references to body products, processes and parts – particularly when they begin potty-training and learn about bodily functions. It's undoubtedly annoying, most definitely childish, but entirely natural.

As young children grow, they become more aware of social and psychological aspects of human interaction and their name-calling will show their new awareness when you hear them using words that are designed to insult – loser, chicken, cow, arsehole, etc. School-age children learn appropriateness when they are intellectually able to appreciate the impact of language on listeners and can empathise with them, but egocentric young children do not fully comprehend why words are offensive to listeners.

But that doesn't mean it is acceptable. Even children who do not understand why or what they are doing can be trained not to use offensive words. Two- and three-year-olds can simply be told never to use a particular word. A five-year-old, however, will need an explanation. An older child of, say, eight, can learn to empathise and understand why words hurt.

Why children swear

Ask a child why he swore. You might be surprised by the answer. Many children simply use the first words that spring to their heads – the types of words they hear on television, or when a parent or sibling is angry. They may express surprise that it is not considered appropriate behaviour. Many children are positively reinforced by siblings or parents to swear. Giving children attention, such as laughing, asking them to repeat a swear word, or even losing the plot completely is enough to encourage the behaviour. Make no mistake. Children of all ages, particularly pre-schoolers, love attention. If they can raise a laugh or even a shouting session with a parent, they'll continue the behaviour. So be careful how you respond.

One common source of swearing is exposure to inappropriate adult role models – either parental figures or adults in the neighbourhood. Popular culture in the form of television, movies, and music lyrics is also a common source of bad language. Children who are allowed access to media without restrictions or supervision are likely to learn and repeat bad language. In some children swearing may be seen as a symptom of underlying, severe psychological problems, such as child abuse or physiological disorders. Meanwhile, children with psychological problems or outbursts of uncontrollable anger may need special attention or counselling. Determining the cause of swearing is the first step to treating it.

What to do

- First of all, it is important to determine what caused the swearing incident in the first place. Is the child seeking attention, bullying another child, or expressing anger? Was the child provoked by another child or was the swearing more spontaneous? You also have to distinguish children who have problems with language from children who have emotional problems with anger or aggression (children who use swearing as a general way to express anger).
- Act quickly when swearing occurs and deal directly with the child who used the bad language.
- Work out the source. Remember that most children begin swearing between the ages of three and five, although children with older siblings may start swearing at an even younger age. Pre-schoolers have a knack for picking up words, especially new ones spoken with any kind of emotion. Eventually, a child is going to blurt out something foul, no matter how sheltered they are. Ask where they heard the word, if they are old enough to understand the question, or look out for bad influences. You can't remove all of them, but you can keep them to a minimum.
- Consider, too, that swearing is a safe way for a child to feel what it is like to be grown up. Children copy grown-ups because it makes them feel grown up. Explain that while some grown-ups swear, nice ones don't and children never do.
- If the child is very young (two to four years) and doesn't understand what he is saying, ignoring the word can work. If swearing persists, then choose a one-line response that's emotionally neutral, such as 'Those are not very nice words to say'.
- If 'potty' language is a regular problem (and remember, a normal development), ask that children only use it in the lavatory. They'll learn that toilet talk belongs in one place only – a little lesson in social etiquette.
- Watch your own mouth. You can't expect children to have a better choice of language than you do. Every time a four-letter word slips out, you are setting a poor example. Sounds easy, but it can be difficult. If you do slip up, apologise.
- Make sure you notice when children show control and find different words. Make them feel clever for finding choices, rather than resorting to swearing, which anyone can do.

Chapter 26: Swearing

- Whenever you hear an offensive word on TV or in public, show disapproval. It's no good ignoring other people's swearing as it will undoubtedly have filtered through. Better to use it as an opportunity to teach something. Interestingly, studies have shown that not reacting to offensive actions around children can cause a significant increase in their antisocial behaviour later.
- If you are a teacher or carer, develop your own code of conduct which you can share with parents. Address unacceptable behaviour and language and make it clear what is expected. If a child learns that he will be in big trouble for using unacceptable words and may be unable to play with his friends, he will learn that his behaviour needs to change.
- Reinforce good language skills by teaching important character-building lessons about respect, reason and responsibility. Children should learn that calling a person a name is both hurtful and disrespectful. The particular word used is a secondary issue; the act of verbally abusing another person is the main problem. Children must learn to take responsibility for the language they use. What you say can get you in trouble at home or at school. Children need to learn that there is a cost to breaking language rules.
- Be a good role model. Don't be caught off guard. Don't over-react or laugh when children swear. What you do when a child sends out a testing bad word may have a lasting impact on the child. When a child swears intentionally or accidentally, work to establish a warm, positive relationship with the child so that he will seek you out for information and advice about words.
- Your goal is to eliminate unacceptable language while at the same time increasing the use of acceptable language. Give rewards in the form of positive comments for children's good speech. 'That was a kind thing to say', or 'What a good choice of words'. Praise is important, but don't go overboard. Over-praise will undo all your good work because nothing will have been learned or earned.
- Outline your expectations: In this house/school/classroom/nursery, we do not use any words that hurt other people or make people unhappy when they hear them.
- Remember that children need to learn which words are bad and which are not. They will not automatically know (although many will have a good idea from the response they get when they use them and the context in which they first heard them). So explain the meaning. Most children are aghast when they understand the meaning of the words they are using and embarrassed to be using them.
- On the same note, establish which words are considered bad in your house or school before you think of correcting the problem. Make it clear why certain words aren't acceptable, regardless of who else uses them. Then be sure that the children know there will be consequences and appropriate discipline for any further use of bad language.
- Some children play well alone but have difficulty suppressing name-calling and bad language when playing with particular classmates. When two children consistently get into trouble together, separate them as much as possible.
- Stay calm. The less irritated you become the more quickly a child will stop using swear words.
- Teach children to express feelings without expletives. Explain the difference between offensive words and expressive words. So it's OK to say abracadabra when you are angry or frustrated because it doesn't offend anyone, but it's not OK to use words that hurt

other people. Ask children to choose different words. Remember that you can't just tell them what not to say, you have to teach them what to say. The next time a child swears, be prepared to give him an alternative word to use instead of just telling him that word is inappropriate.

- Teach absolute NO words. This is particularly important with very young children who will not understand why words are not acceptable. We do not use that word. It is a bad word. End of story.
- Maintain your composure. If you react violently or with anger, a child may well see this as a form of attention. Use the same line over and over again; for example: 'I do not like those words,' every time a child swears.
- Be realistic. Even young children can develop bad habits when it comes to swearing. Unless they are absolutely convinced that their use won't be rewarded with attention, they will not stop. Give the habit time to disappear. Just remain calm and consistent.

Some swearing is common in most children and a part of normal development. However, remember that it is experimentation on their part and needs to be quashed as soon as possible. Very young children can simply be trained not to use offensive words, while older children will need to have the reasons why they are offensive explained. Teaching alternative forms of expression, modelling good behaviour and outlining expectations, with penalties for breaking the rules, should always be undertaken by carers.

Most importantly, stay calm. If a child learns that using an emotive word will get attention you can bet they'll use it again and again. Remove influences, of any nature, that you think might be contributing to the problem and use the episode as a springboard for teaching good manners and kindness. No one has to swear; teach children the alternatives.

Key points

- Swearing is a normal part of child development and usually begins around the ages of three to five, or earlier in children with older siblings.
- Most children do not understand what they are saying or why it is offensive; take the time to explain why words hurt or offend other people.
- Teach alternative ways of expressing anger and frustration. A wide vocabulary can help to curb the problem.
- Always be calm and refrain from swearing yourself. Apologise if you slip up, and ensure that you never reinforce negative behaviours by laughing or over-reacting.
- Watch a child's influences. If swearing continues, despite a policy to discontinue it, try to work out where it is coming from and eliminate the source when possible.

Chapter 27

Talking back

As frustrating and enraging as talking back can be, it is a normal part of a young child's development, and is to some extent fostered by the youth culture that is portrayed in the media.

While understanding the reasons behind back-talk is important, it is equally crucial that this type of behaviour is replaced with courtesy in the context of a strong code of discipline. An obnoxious, rude child will feel empowered through the reaction he gets, and develop an unhealthy attitude towards authority figures and rules, which can have a dramatic effect on behaviour patterns later in life. We talked about cheeky children on page 45; remember: a little spirit is fine, as is a good sense of humour. But cheeky can often cross the line into rudeness, and talking back is a prime example of that.

It is important to remember that during the early pre-school years, children's language skills are rapidly growing and they begin to recognise the impact of their own words. When words elicit a strong response from others, this can be a powerful experience for a young child. Also, while young children are able to experience a wide range of emotions, they do not typically have the advanced language skills to fully express their feelings. Back-talk at this age may be a child's attempt to verbalise some of the very powerful feelings that he is experiencing.

Furthermore, pre-school children and those who are just starting school are beginning to exert their independence, and one way of showing that they are separate beings with feelings and opinions of their own is to express them constantly and to disagree with anyone who seems to be capable of standing in the way of their perceived needs. There are plenty of changes afoot in this age group, and children often attempt to control their world by setting it up exactly as they wish it to be. Any attempt by a parent or carer to suggest an alternative route is firmly discounted and the focus of often belligerent talking back.

Youth culture today, even with children as young as two or three, seems to be cheekier and perhaps more argumentative than in past generations. Children see attitude on TV, and watch children ruling the roost and demanding respect and rights. Laughter greets back-talk – to parents, siblings and other children – so, not surprisingly, young children pick this up and mimic it. Older siblings, too, feed the trend. It is difficult to tone down rude behaviour when it is so all pervasive.

What can you do?

When a child experiences strong emotions, he needs to learn to express himself and his feelings in more appropriate ways. Teaching verbal expression is a cornerstone of discipline because it allows children to find acceptable ways to get their point and their feelings across without being disrespectful. Children need to learn that experiencing emotions such as frustration, anger, jealousy and even hatred are normal and acceptable, but that they need to be expressed in different terms. In other words, talking back politely, by putting forward a view, expressing an opinion, making a request or explaining feelings is fine, but being belligerent, rude and argumentative is not. It's the words that count, not the feelings.

Watch television with your children and comment on rude back-talk, making it clear that you find it unacceptable. Be as firm with older children in your care as you are with the little ones, so that everyone understands where you stand on the issue.

Try to explain to children that back-talk is hurtful, rude and upsetting, and that although it may be funny to see on television, in real life it is not acceptable to behave like that. Even young children can understand the concept that television is not real life, and it is a point you need to make abundantly clear.

As challenging as it may be, it is important to remain calm during periods of back-talk. Maintaining this sense of calm will help defuse the situation, help your child regain his composure and minimise the power of angry words. Young children have not mastered the subtle nuances of language. 'I hate you' to a four-year-old may actually mean: 'I was having fun and I didn't want to stop playing.' Do not take his words personally. His outbursts are likely to be the result of feeling overwhelmed by a situation and being unable to fully express his feelings.

Top tips

- Set an example for children in daily life. One of the ways they will learn how to express a wide range of emotions appropriately is by watching you, whether you are a parent, a teacher or a carer. You have plenty of everyday opportunities to model verbal expression of feelings and other effective coping strategies. For example, if someone is rude to you, it is important to explain that you feel hurt and angry, but that you know that talking back to this person will just start an argument that will leave everyone feeling unhappy and upset. Rude behaviour is all around us – unfortunately a feature of a society overwhelmed by stress and anger. How we deal with it – whether it is negotiating with an irate parent, a driver on the road, a shop assistant or a rude teenager on the street – teaches children how to respond when they are confronted, and when things do not go their way.
- It does not matter whether your child is five, ten or fifteen years old, the way to deal with back-talk is the same for all ages. Back-talk is designed to get a response from grown-ups; therefore, the most effective way to respond to it is calmly. If a child gets no response, time after time, the behaviour will diminish.
- Acknowledge a child's feelings by saying something like: 'You must be very upset and angry. Why don't we talk about it once you've calmed down?'
- Be responsive, not reactive, because the greater the reaction, the greater the appeal. Calmly ask a child to express himself politely and do not respond until he does. 'I will consider your request when you can talk to me without that attitude.'

- Remember that engaging in back-talk yourself simply leads to a power struggle, and teaches children that it is the best way to get what they want. Power struggles have a habit of going on and on and on....
- Defuse the situation. Children communicate through their behaviour, particularly when they are too young to find the words to express themselves verbally. Ask yourself what is really going on – why is the child angry or upset, or taking a stand? Try to see things from a child's perspective and appreciate frustration that leads to inappropriate language. If you can deal with the underlying problem, you will teach children to do the same.
- Encourage children to think about words before they use them. Stop them in their tracks if they start to talk back, and ask them to take a break and to continue more reasonably. Even young children can pick up appropriate behaviour. Give a visual cue, such as holding your hand in the air when you think their actions or their words are unacceptable.
- Do not fall into defending yourself against the old 'it's not fair' routine. Most children feel a huge sense of injustice when things do not go exactly as they have planned, and genuinely do think they have been mistreated or given short shrift. The only sane response is to agree with the child – 'Yes, it's not fair that you have to stop playing when you are having fun, but we have to tidy up and have lunch.' Or: 'Yes it's not fair that your brother has a new toy and you do not, but there are other times when you have one and he does not.' End of discussion. You've acknowledged the emotion, but you are not prepared to negotiate. Most children will not be hugely thrilled with this type of explanation, but if you repeat it every time that he begins an 'it's not fair' session, eventually he will see that you are sticking to your guns and arguing about it is only a waste of time.
- Use the word 'no' wisely – consider a request before you lay down the law, and avoid saying 'no' for things that simply are not important. Distract a child with something else, or suggest an alternative without actually saying that they cannot do or continue something they wish. Use 'no' for important issues, such as safety and household rules, and teach your child to negotiate calmly and politely for things that are really important to them. But when you have said 'no', it is essential that you stick to it.
- No argumentative stage will go away until you make it very clear that you will not accept it, that there will be consequences and that you expect civility in the household, nursery or classroom.
- If children remain less than respectful, tend to argue at the drop of the hat or always seem to have to get in the last word, set up some clear guidelines. You cannot expect young children to know instinctively how to behave, so you will have to outline your expectations, explain why different behaviours are appropriate and others are not, and then enforce the positive behaviours you want to see, while clamping down on the behaviours you find unacceptable. A good way to do this is the age-old star chart – good behaviour is rewarded.
- You can also consider a 'demerit' system, where talking back is noted on the blackboard or on a chart on the wall. A set number of demerits has a prearranged consequence. You may find that many children will push and push to the edge of their limit, but then stop just before a penalty is about to be imposed. This does, however, show some self-control and this is the type of behaviour you wish to foster.

The most successful way of nipping back-talk in the bud is to set out a clear agenda for children – explaining what you expect from them in terms of behaviour, and what you find acceptable. There needs to be a 'no-tolerance' policy in place, in which you consistently refuse to discuss or negotiate with a young child who is behaving inappropriately.

Give children choices to ensure that they do not feel powerless, but be firm and calm when they do not make the right choices. Eventually all children will see that talking back will get them nowhere, and that if they want their perceived needs met, they have to learn to negotiate calmly, explain how they are feeling using appropriate words and tone of voice and accept 'no' for an answer.

It is not an easy lesson to learn, as it may be the first time that they have their new feelings of independence threatened, but all children need to learn the bounds of acceptable and respectful behaviour. Consistently rewarding the behaviour you want to see while penalising what you find unacceptable may seem obvious, but it does work in the short and long term.

You can't make me!

'You can't make me!' is another common form of back-talk – and it tends to come from children who feel a need to be in charge, and see any form of authority as an attempt to undermine them. They say no before they have even had time to process a request.

The real answer is that you need to assert your own authority. Children can certainly have views, opinions and wishes, but ultimately they also need to learn that you make the rules and you uphold them.

There are several good ways to deal with this. First of all, be consistent. If you give in once, they will continue to behave in the same way every time in the hope that you will give in again. Secondly, offer some choices and consequences.

For example, 'If you don't put away your books now (or when the timer goes, when lunch is ready or when the video has finished), there will be no playtime after lunch/no trip to the park or there will be a time-out or a trip to the naughty cushion or step'. This gives children very clear choices. They need to feel some control over their actions, and by giving them the clear consequence (which will be calmly and consistently applied), they will learn, eventually, to make wiser choices.

Remember, never try to reason with the unreasonable. Young children are very self-absorbed and often unreasonable, and to expect children to see things your way may well be unreasonable, too. Ending a game they are enjoying, clearing up after themselves, going out to do the shopping or even changing activities may not be high on their agenda, but if you make it clear that you are sticking to your guns, they will eventually concede that you can make them do things.

The secret is, of course, to avoid locking horns by giving clear choices and consequences. Children choose the behaviour and pay the consequences, so they are empowered and feel that they have a modicum of control, and no real reason to lose face by giving in.

Key points

- Back-talk is a normal part of development, in which children learn to express the strong feelings they have.
- Back-talk continues when children get a response because it makes them feel powerful.
- Parents, carers and teachers must model the behaviour they wish to see in children. Engaging in a sparring match simply teaches children to fight back and hold their corner.
- Look for the motivation behind the words and address the cause rather than just the sassy talk.
- Lay out your expectations and remain firm. Giving in once will cause a cycle of back-talk and power struggle.
- Give children choices and consequences, so that they learn that their actions and the way they speak have an impact.
- Use the word 'no' sensibly.

Chapter 28

Tantrums

Even the best-behaved young children will complain, argue, hit and rebel from time to time and when frustration hits a peak, they will succumb to temper tantrums. While tantrums can be embarrassing, challenging and distressing for parents, teachers and carers, they are a normal part of development for young children. With a little understanding and a firm hand, however, they can be dealt with quickly and effectively, and in the process many children will begin to understand how to express themselves in a more positive way.

The average young child will experience between one and two temper tantrums a week between the ages of one and four, and they are equally common in boys and girls. Some children 'tantrum' more frequently, a situation that can spiral out of control if measures are not taken to get to the root of the problem. It is important to remember that a 'tantrumming' child is not bad or naughty, but is using his behaviour in an attempt to communicate his feelings.

Most parents are aware of typical situations that act as triggers for tantrums – for example bedtime, mealtimes, getting dressed, watching television, when parents are on the telephone or when there are visitors to the house. In a school or nursery environment playtime is often a catalyst, as are periods when activities change or a carer or teacher is occupied with another child or activity.

The causes of tantrums

Some experts call the classic temper tantrum period early adolescence, as a struggle for independence is often at the root of the problem. From 18 months to about four years, children will struggle to make themselves and their perceived needs heard, but because their emotional vocabularies and their problem-solving skills tend to be limited, they decline into a blue mist of frustration and anger that manifests itself as a tantrum. According to Robert G. Harrington, PhD, a professor in the Department of Psychology and Research in Education at the University of Kansas, who wrote a key paper on tantrums for the National Association of School Psychologists in the US, there are several key stages at which tantrums occur, and each has a unique cause:

18 months to two years of age:

Children during this stage will test the limits. They want to see how far they can go before a parent or caretaker stops their behaviour. At the age of two children are very egocentric; they cannot see another person's point of view. They want independence to explore their environment. When the child cannot reach a goal, he shows his frustration by crying, arguing, yelling or hitting.

Chapter 28: Tantrums

When the child's need for independence collides with the adult's need for safety, conformity, or getting on with the task at hand, the conditions are perfect for a power struggle and a temper tantrum. The child's goal, of course, is to get the adult to give in or get out of the way. What is most upsetting to caregivers is that it is virtually impossible to reason with a child who is having a temper tantrum. Thus, arguing and cajoling in response to a temper tantrum only escalates the problem.

Three- and four-year-olds:
By the time children reach three to four, many of them are less impulsive and they can use language to express their needs. Tantrums at this age are often less frequent and less severe. Nevertheless, some pre-schoolers have learnt that a temper tantrum is a good way to get what they want.

Four-year-olds:
By the age of four, most children will have completed, and most caregivers will have survived, the tantrum phase. By this age, children have attained the necessary motor and physical skills to meet many of their own needs without relying so much on adults. Their growing language skills allow them to express their anger, to problem-solve and to compromise.

Forces

Despite these improved skills, nursery, kindergarten and primary school-age children can still have temper tantrums when faced with demanding academic tasks or new interpersonal situations in school or at home. Sue Dinwiddie, an American lecturer who deals with conflict resolution in families, breaks tantrums into three main 'forces':

Manipulative tantrums occur when the child does not get his own way. They will stop when they are ignored. The child erupts, the parent or carer calmly walks away. Before long the tantrum subsides, and the child sobs in contrition. Some parents and carers prefer to remove the child from the scene. 'When you have finished with your tantrum, you may come back and join us.' Young children don't actually plot out, 'OK, I'm not getting my own way, so I'll throw a fit.' They fall apart without thinking. But if the parent gives in to stop the tantrum, the behaviour is rewarded and reinforced, leading to tantrum blackmail.

Verbal frustration tantrums occur when the child knows what he wants but lacks the verbal skills to communicate clearly. Frustration boils over, and the drama begins. Ignoring these tantrums makes the child even more frustrated. Verbal frustration tantrums subside as children's communication skills improve.

Temperamental tantrums occur when the child's frustration level reaches the rage stage, and he becomes totally out of control, falling apart emotionally. The child may be too tired or tremendously disappointed. As with verbal frustration tantrums, temperamental tantrums are seldom cured by ignoring. The child can rarely gain control alone. Feeling irritable, cross and excitable is scary, confusing and disorienting for children. It is difficult to concentrate and to regain control.

So what can you do?

The most important thing that any carer, teacher or parent can do is to prevent tantrums well before they set in. Learn to recognise the triggers and step in. One of the most important things anyone looking after small children can do is to remember that tantrums are normally the product of frustration. If an adult gives a child the vocabulary he needs, a show of understanding and empathy, but also exercises a clear and firm policy regarding discipline, the child will learn both to understand himself, to gauge situations, and to react in a more positive manner.

Here are some of the best ways to avoid tantrums:

- Always focus on positive rather than negative behaviour, so that the child learns that he will get attention by behaving well rather than having to resort to drama and aggression. This sounds simplistic, but we often fail to notice and reward the good things that children do throughout the day, and concentrate our energies on dealing with things when they go wrong.
- Giving children choices is an important part of helping them to grow up making decisions for themselves, and it can be an important tool for getting through a situation when a child is inclined to dig in his heels. He'll also feel more in control because you have empowered him by allowing him to make some decisions of his own, which shows some respect. 'Do you want to put the books away or the trains?', 'Do you want to sit on the chair or on the floor?', 'Shall we use the mugs or the red cups for juice?'. The message is that the decision has been made by you regarding the activity. However, the little choices along the way make it possible for a child to acquiesce without losing face at a time when he is exercising some independence. A word of caution, however: do not offer choices where there are none. You'll create the scenario for a battle and the inevitable tantrum.
- If there are items that you don't want a child to use, play with or have at a certain time (for example scissors or a teddy bear that you reserve for night-time), keep them well out of sight. Setting yourself up for a battle, or making a point, will not teach a child anything other than the fact that you are more powerful. It's an invitation to lock horns.
- Distraction is one of the best methods any carer can use with small children. If you see an argument brewing, change the room, scene or activity immediately. Children are easily distracted and will forget the cause of their fury if you step in quickly.
- Take care not to battle over everything. Save the word 'no' for important issues, such as safety and predetermined household rules. If a child feels powerless, he'll take steps to ensure that you know where he stands, and that's an instant recipe for trouble. Use potentially problematic situations as an opportunity to teach your child something. If he demands a toy and goes into a strop until you get it, gently suggest that he asks politely. If he can do this, and continue to ask politely for things he wants, then try to honour the request from time to time.
- Remember that tired children are much more likely to respond negatively to trigger situations, and they are also more likely to act up when they are hungry. Try to plan activities for periods when a child is well rested and fed.

- Remember that boredom and frustration are common triggers for tantrums. Don't push a child past his attention span or insist that he finish a project (for example a jigsaw) if he's bored or finding it difficult.
- All children need some freedom to explore and to exercise their imaginations and new skills. If you are overly worried about safety, hygiene and rules, a child will never have the opportunity he needs to learn about his environment and to grow physically, intellectually and emotionally. Give him some free rein from time to time and ensure that your environment is safe enough for him to explore without getting into trouble.
- Allow children to make mistakes. Picking up on every single potential problem will just leave a child disheartened and unwilling to try anything for fear of getting it wrong. Mistakes are part of the learning process, and you must exercise some patience. Furthermore, a child who believes he is in trouble no matter what he does will make no effort to behave more positively – and the crimes are likely to become more serious when he believes that he is naughty. Why not? If he's going to be punished for taking another child's biscuit, why not break a window if the reaction is much the same? Keep things in perspective.
- Remember the importance of routines. All children respond better to situations when they know where they stand. Plot out their day for them in advance, so that they can anticipate what happens next. For example, bedtime is never as much of a battle when a firm routine is in place, beginning with a bath, a cuddle, a story and a chat. A well-structured day, in the classroom or at home, adds an element of predictability to a child's life and he is less likely to feel out of control and out of sorts.
- Give notice when activities are going to change. Turning off a favourite video without warning is like a red rag to a bull. Preparing children for transition, by showing them the numbers on a clock, or giving them a pre-defined time space (when the bell rings, when the baby wakes up, when mummy gets home) helps them to manage change more easily.
- Provide learning, behavioural, and social activities which are at the child's developmental level so that he does not become either frustrated or easily bored. Children should be ready for new experiences so that they face challenge without undue difficulty.
- Remember to keep your sense of humour – there is nothing more absurd than a two-year-old standing up to a fully-grown man or woman. Sometimes laughter is the best diversion.
- Teach children to recognise signs of an impending tantrum. This is a skill that will set them in good stead for the rest of their lives, as they learn to communicate and control their own emotions before they blow. When they look angry, ask them how they are feeling or what they are thinking. Give them solutions – 'If you feel angry, do you think it would be a good idea to run around the garden for a few minutes until you feel a little better?' 'If this game is making you cross, shall we just put it away?' 'If your friend is determined to have that toy, shall we just let him have it and find something different to do?'
- Give children words to express their anger constructively, and teach them to avoid power struggles by reminding them that you will listen to their problems when they are calm and can express themselves calmly. Suggest words that will help a child to understand how he is feeling: confused, angry, hurt, frustrated, bored, jealous. Ask him

to come up with ways to deal with his feelings, and suggest others. Tell him stories about how you felt in a similar situation, and how you dealt with those feelings.
- Don't hesitate to use creative efforts to encourage children to express their feelings: painting 'angry' or 'sad' can help a young child get things out of his system; dancing to loud or gentle music; stretching; imagining wonderful calm places together or even telling stories to one another can help.

In the throes of a tantrum

- It might help to work out what type of tantrum your child is having, in order to deal with it in the best possible way. For manipulative tantrums, the best thing to do is to ignore the behaviour. This can be difficult when there are other children about, or if you are out of the nursery or household environment. However, a child does need to learn that attention is not on the agenda if he behaves that way. Be firm. Explain why you are not acquiescing to a request.
- Above all, do not worry about what other people think. If they haven't been through this ordeal, they haven't had children. And if they gave in to a tantrumming child's demands, they are likely to be the proud owners of manipulative tyrants.
- You can offer choices: stop this behaviour now and we will, for example, remain in the park or continue to play trains. Don't enter into a long-winded negotiation. No child in the throes of a tantrum is capable of calm negotiation.
- For tantrums brought on by verbal frustration, don't ignore your child as he will feel even more frustrated. Validate the anger by helping your child label his feelings. Then problem-solve together. You may have to guess at the cause, but don't give up.
- Give your child words and solutions so that he knows how to deal with these kinds of feelings in the future. Verbal frustration tantrums subside as children's communication skills improve.
- Temperamental tantrums usually occur when a child is too tired, hungry or disappointed to think rationally. Try to stay calm yourself (modelling calm behaviour is essential in all tantrum situations) and then validate your child's feelings, encouraging him to express them.
- Offer an acceptable alternative: I know you want sweets, but we are having healthy food before dinner. Do you want a banana or some raisins?
- A child who is out of control often needs physical reassurance, and a hug can make a big difference. This may be difficult in a nursery environment, but encourage a child under these circumstances to find a soft toy and give it a good squeeze. Encourage a child to take deep breaths, or to have a little run around the garden or playground. Express your understanding and reiterate the fact that you are there to help, and that you can help. Books, songs, jokes can distract a child from his feelings and the problem to hand.

For all tantrums

- Think before you act. Count to ten and then think about the source of the child's frustration, this child's characteristic response to stress (for example hyperactivity, distractibility or moodiness) and the predictable steps that will be likely to escalate the tantrum.

- Next, try to intervene before the child is out of control. Get down at the child's eye level and say: 'You are starting to lose control, slow down.' You can now use distraction techniques.
- Some children respond well to time out, simply as a means of giving them some space to collect themselves and to avoid losing face when they feel out of control. Don't suggest it as a punishment, but as a quiet place where a child can go to calm down.
- Ignore the tantrum if they are throwing it to get your attention. Once they calm down, give them the attention they desire.
- Whatever means you choose, remember that a child in the throes of a tantrum is out of control and probably feeling unlovable. Even in the depths of rage, he will still fear losing your love or respect, and it's important to reassure him that you respect, love or admire him, no matter how he is behaving.
- Never give in to a tantrum under any circumstances. That response will only escalate the intensity and frequency of temper tantrums.
- Do not reward the child once he has calmed down after a tantrum. Some children will learn that a temper tantrum is a good way to get a treat later.
- Don't hesitate to talk about the tantrum after it has passed. Encourage your child to express how he was feeling and help him to come up with better ways to deal with those feelings. Use it as an opportunity to teach a child something, and to give him the tools he needs to make better choices in future. Ignoring it makes it seem much more sinister than it needs to be, and a child may end up feeling embarrassed and negative about himself.

All children will have tantrums from time to time, but a little prevention goes a long way towards warding them off. Adults, too, feel frustrated and out of control from time to time, so it's not surprising that children, who lack the emotional sophistication of adults, lose their cool and act up. Avoid situations where tantrums are likely to occur, focus on positive behaviour, and use a tantrum as an opportunity to teach your child something about his emotions, and the positive ways that can be implemented to deal with them.

Key points

- Children between the ages of one and four will have an average of one to two tantrums per week, tailing off as a child becomes older. Girls and boys are equally liable to have tantrums.
- A strong routine helps a child to feel more secure and less easily upset by problems that arise throughout his day.
- There are three main types of tantrum: manipulative, temperamental and verbal frustration. Try to work out the cause of a child's tantrum before dealing with it. Ignoring is often best, if a child is trying to get attention.
- Always validate a child's feelings and offer him choices so that he feels more in control and empowered within his own environment.
- Do not give in to tantrums, because it only increases their frequency.

Further Reading

A number of books for children are noted throughout this book, and will encourage a child to understand better both what he is feeling and experiencing, and how a positive outcome can be achieved. Other good books to consider for children include:

Hodder Wayland's 'Your Emotions' series – lots of different books, including *I Feel Angry, I Feel Frightened, I Feel Sad*, and much, much more.

Hodder Wayland publishes a 'Your Feelings' series, which includes many excellent books, such as *It's Not Fair, I'm Worried, I'm Shy* and *I Feel Bullied*. Try the 'Values' series by the same publisher, with books such as *It Wasn't ME!: Learning About Honesty, Excuse ME: Learning About Politeness*, and *I Don't Care!: Learning About Respect*. Their MYBees series is also good for slightly older children: *Stop Picking on Me!* is a good example.

Or try Usborne's 'Cautionary Tales' series, which teaches some important lessons through exciting stories such as *Give That Back, Jack, Don't be a Bully, Billy!* and *Don't Tell Lies, Lucy!*

Hands are not for Hitting by Martine Agassi is an American title, but easily obtained in the UK through Amazon and other internet retailers. *Teeth are Not for Biting, Words are Not for Hurting*, and *Feet are Not for Kicking* are other books in an excellent series.

The 'All Kinds of' series, published by Tango has *All Kinds of Feelings* by Emma Brownjohn, which is a good starter for emotional literacy and expression.

For adults

Good titles that you may want to pick up are:

Caring for Your Baby and Young Child: Birth to Age 5, by The American Academy of Pediatrics, Bantam.

Commonsense Healthcare for Children by Karen Sullivan (Piatkus).

From Birth to Five Years: Children's Developmental Progress by Mary D. Sheridan, Marion Frost (Editor), Ajay Sharma (Editor) (Routledge).

How to Say No and Mean It by Karen Sullivan (HarperCollins).

No-Cry Sleep Solution for Toddlers and Preschoolers by Elizabeth Pantley (McGraw-Hill).

Positive Discipline for Pre-schoolers, Ages 3-6 by Jane Nelsen (Prima).

Raising Boys and Raising Girls by Steve Biddulph (HarperCollins) are both good titles to see you through the pre-school years.

Further Reading

The Best Friends' Guide to Toddlers: A Survival Manual to the 'Terrible Twos' (and Ones and Threes) from the First Step, the First Potty and the First Word ('No') to the Last Blanket, by Vicki Iovine (Bloomsbury).

The Pocket Parent by Gail Reichlin, Caroline Winkler (Workman).

The Toddler's Busy Book: 365 Creative Games and Activities to Keep Your One and a Half to Three Year-old Busy by Trish Kuffner (Meadowbrook).

Theories of Childhood: An Introduction to Dewey, Montessori, Erickson, Piaget and Vygotsky by Carol Garhart Mooney (Redleaf) – an invaluable and easy-to-read guide to child development theory.

Toddler Taming or Toddler Taming Tips, by Dr Christopher Green (Vermilion).

Understanding Your Two-Year-Old by Lisa Miller is just one title in the 'Understanding Your Child' series, which takes you right up to teens (Jessica Kingsley Publishers).

What to Expect: The Toddler Years by Arlene Eisenberg, Heidi E. Murkoff, Sandee E. Hathaway (Simon & Schuster).

Books to read with children

These are books which I have mentioned in the main text.

Being Jealous by Sarah Levete (Copper Beech Books).

Big Ernie's New Home by Teresa Martin and Whitney Martin

Breakfast with the Bears by Patti Jennings and Poppy Wells.

Can't You Sleep Little Bear? by Martin Waddell.

Did You Think I Would Leave You Crying? by Moira Miller.

I Feel Angry by Brian Moses and Mike Gordon, published by Hodder Wayland.

I Feel Jealous by Brian Moses (Hodder Wayland).

I'm Shy by Karen Bryant-Mole.

Little Miss Shy by Roger Hargreaves.

Miffy Is Crying by Dick Bruna.

Further Reading

Mine by Miriam Cohen,

Mine, Mine, Mine! A Little Help With Sharing by Sheryl Berk and Josie Yess

My New Baby, by Annie Kubler

Poemotions: Poems about Being Angry - I Want to Shout and Stamp About by Tony Mitton and Mike Gordon published by Hodder Children's Books.

Poems about Being Scared by Brian Moses and Mike Gordon

Rosie's First Day at School (Talking it Through) by Rosemary Stones

Share Said the Rooster by Pamela Allen

Shy Sophie by Tony Garth

The Owl Who Was Afraid of the Dark by Jill Tomlinson and Paul Howard.

When I Feel Afraid by Cheri J Meiners and Meredith Johnson.

When I'm Feeling Scared by Trace Moroney

Why Should I Share? by Clare Llewellyn and Mike Gordon.